Teacher
Portfolios

Teacher Portfolios
Literacy Artifacts and Themes

Sheri Everts Rogers
Kathy Everts Danielson

HEINEMANN
Portsmouth, NH

HEINEMANN
A division of Reed Elsevier Inc.
361 Hanover Street
Portsmouth, NH 03801-3912

Offices and agents throughout the world

Library of Congress Cataloging-in-Publication Data

Rogers, Sheri Everts.
    Teacher portfolios : literacy artifacts and themes / Sheri Everts
  Rogers, Kathy Everts Danielson.
      p.   cm.
    Includes bibliographical references.
    ISBN 0-435-08881-5
    1. English language—Rhetoric—Study and teaching—Theory, etc.
  2. English teachers—Training of.   3. Portfolios in education.
  4. Literacy.   I. Danielson, Kathy Everts.   II. Title.
PE1404.R62   1996   96-28883
                                       CIP

Editor: Leigh Peake
Production: Vicki Kasabian
Book design: Joni Doherty
Cover design: Barbara Whitehead
Manufacturing: Louise Richardson

Printed in the United States of America on acid-free paper

99 98 97 96 EB 1 2 3 4 5

Contents

Preface

The widespread adoption of portfolios for student assessment is important. Yet, until teachers themselves keep portfolios that document who they are as readers and writers, portfolios probably will continue to be merely folders in which teachers place students' work that they have selected to show to parents or to document student achievement. It is our belief that portfolios can be used much more effectively if teachers have a better understanding of the process of keeping a portfolio themselves. When teachers feel ownership of portfolios, students are more apt to as well.

We require our students to keep portfolios, and we keep them too, modeling the process of collecting, selecting, and reflecting. We wrote this book so that our students and other preservice and inservice teachers could see the many possibilities of portfolios. Moreover, we needed an example of a portfolio for our students that wasn't ours. We could provide examples from other students, but that would be just one model. We wanted to give our students a sense of the range of possibilities for portfolios and some notion of the depth they would need to provide for themselves.

In this book we have tried to represent the range of achievement that portfolios can illustrate for individuals. The message should be that a portfolio and its artifacts are *uniquely* individual. We have collected some ideas others have had—things that have made sense for them and that best illustrate what reflective, talented learners teachers are. We hope these examples will allow you to go and make those same decisions on your own. Because while this book seeks to introduce the reader to the possibilities of keeping a portfolio, there is no substitute for keeping one yourself.

Acknowledgments

We would like to thank the children and preservice and inservice teachers who allowed us to use artifacts from their portfolios for this book. We have learned a great deal about portfolios from and with our students at the University of Nebraska at Omaha, and we thank them.

We would also like to thank our editor at Heinemann, Leigh Peake, with whom we have shared many delightful conference calls.

We would also like to thank a magnificent assistant, Tammy Murphy, who helped with the transfer of the artifacts to disk.

And finally, we would like to thank and dedicate this book to our mother, who continues to value all eight of her diverse children.

1 | Getting Started with Portfolios

As mentioned in the preface, we require our students (preservice and inservice teachers) to keep portfolios. We keep portfolios right along with them, modeling the processes of collection, selection, and reflection. This book was written to provide some examples of literacy artifacts kept by our students and ourselves. We firmly believe that teachers must keep portfolios too if they ask their students to do so. When teachers feel ownership of the portfolio process, students are more apt to as well.

Kathy's Perspective

Portfolios were first used by artists to showcase their achievement and skills. They provide real evidence of a person's quality of work through a selection of appropriate work samples.

Rief (1992) suggested that in order for portfolios to be authentic assessment, students must be immersed in reading, writing, speaking, and listening. They must also be given choices about what they are doing and must receive positive responses to their ideas.

The *value* aspect of evaluation is also important. Students should see the portfolio as a reflection of themselves as learners and should celebrate their accomplishments.

Ultimately, evaluation should be a celebration. Joint evaluation with the children more clearly gives us cause to celebrate. We take risks. We achieve objectives. We rejoice together. (Graves 1991, 187)

In keeping portfolios with her eighth-grade students, Linda Rief reiterates this value notion of evaluation.

I want to show the possibilities in diversity, depth, growth, and self-evaluation. This kind of evidence shows the value in evaluation. This kind of assessment *matters*. (Rief 1992, 47)

Teachers should also keep portfolios, not only to model the process, but also to fully understand the process of assessment. Graves suggests the importance of the teacher modeling the portfolio process in this way:

Evaluation in my classroom, however, must begin with a careful assessment of my own literate engagement. I cannot expect of children what I do not practice myself. I simply won't see the opportunities for children to exercise responsibility if I am not aware from my own practice what is involved in the process. (Graves 1991, 187)

Graves also sees the importance of policy makers truly understanding the process of portfolios:

As I travel across the country and speak with various professionals engaged in portfolio study, I am surprised to find that many have not kept portfolios themselves. They are not unlike professionals who teach writing without writing themselves. They are unacquainted with the actual process of making decisions about what to include in a portfolio from their own work, and they are unfamiliar with the heady moment of sharing one's work with students or another professional.

From the outside, the process of maintaining a portfolio appears to be a simple task, uncomplicated by strong emotions or tough thinking. We need more policy makers, administrators, and teachers who know portfolios *from the inside*. Their decisions about portfolio use must include the reality of living and growing with the process of keeping one. (Graves 1992, 5)

Portfolios must be kept by teachers, too, if the value of evaluation is to be truly considered. Teachers must see themselves as readers, writers, and learners also. Students need literate role models from which to learn.

Introducing Portfolios

In my undergraduate reading/language arts methods class (as well as my graduate classes), I share my portfolio with the class on the first day. I tell them that this is my portfolio as of this day, but it will change throughout the year, just as I change as a reader, writer, and learner.

I tell them my section headings and the types of things I have included in my portfolio. I then give them the requirements for their portfolios and I also give them a handout of ideas of things they could also include in their portfolios (Figures 1–1 and 1–2). Throughout the semester we brainstorm other items that could be added to the portfolio.

Invariably, students ask how these portfolios will be graded. It is at this point that I share with them the rubric that we developed (Figure 1–3).

To get started with the portfolio, I ask students to think about who they are as readers, writers, and learners. I then encourage them to make their portfolio unique to reflect themselves as learners. Photographs, Post-It notes, quotes, and other ways of representing themselves are discussed as we all learn from each other.

At the end of the semester, when students share their final draft of the portfolio with me, we reflect on the portfolio experiences together. Questions that we use to guide this discussion appear in Figure 1–4. We also determine the student's grade together. Their self-assessment is an important part of the portfolio. Many have never given themselves a grade before, and this gives them a chance to truly think about the effort, time, and learning that took place throughout the portfolio. This type of reflection helps them plan for future reading, writing, and learning.

Throughout the semester, we are readers, writers, listeners, and speakers. We begin our class with Sustained Silent Reading time. Students read anything of their choice, and I always have a bin of books for anyone who needs something to read. We also write every day in class. I often give students a prompt, but they are encouraged to write about whatever they want in their writing notebooks. Often these rough drafts or ideas are transformed into a further draft, a poem, a letter to the editor, etc. Students speak and listen every day as well. All students give a presentation, either telling us a story with props or demonstrating how to make something. As listeners we learn from one another. As speakers we learn appropriate ways of involving one another. As learners we find out that we need to have students involved with their own learning if they are to take responsibility and ownership for their own literacy. The portfolio is then a means for showing how we have all learned in our own unique, individual ways. Portfolios are a way to say who we are as readers, writers, listeners, speakers, and learners.

Just as we learn to read by reading and we learn to write by writing, we learn about portfolios by keeping them ourselves. Teachers must also keep portfolios, not only to model the process for students, but to grow themselves as readers and writers. This type of assessment is meaningful, and it matters.

Sheri's Perspective

"Jane Hansen likes to say that a portfolio ought to show who we are and who want to be" (Sunstein 1992, xii). That is the purpose of a portfolio—to show who we are now and who we want to be as teachers, as learners. Just as artists keep portfolios of their best and ongoing work, a portfolio should be a reflection of our current and emerging selves. A portfolio provides an opportunity for each individual to shine, to share what matters to them, to illustrate what it is that makes each individual so delightfully unique. There is no right or wrong way to construct a portfolio. There are only possibilities, varying degrees of depth and width.

Keeping portfolios, like everything in else in life, seemingly, is best learned by doing. As I tell my children when they are faced with something they have never done and don't think they can do: Pretend that you can. You'll learn as you go. You'll learn as you make mistakes. You'll learn as you begin to see benefits, limitations, and questions. However, you'll only learn these aspects if you, too, are keeping a portfolio. For me, it is akin to coaching. We wouldn't think of hiring a football coach who had never played the game. A coach who has never played the game doesn't understand the pitfalls, the ins and outs, the shortcuts, and the strategies one must employ to be successful. The same holds true with portfolios. You have to keep one to understand why it is important to keep one. And only through maintaining a portfolio can we understand the questions our students will have, or begin to understand "who we are and who we want to be."

Introducing Portfolios: Collection, Selection, Reflection, and Projection

Collection   I like to introduce portfolios by using actual portfolios I have compiled for varied purposes. I have several portfolios in varying states of readiness and I share those with my students. I continue to share those portfolios throughout the course of the year because, as a student told me recently, "I wasn't ready to see it at the beginning. I can finally understand what it means, but only now." Different students will need to see a portfolio at unique times throughout their processes. Some only need to talk about the processes involved (collection, selection, reflection, and projection) and they are on their way. Others need to hear ideas daily. I share artifacts I am collecting on a daily basis in the early going. I keep a new portfolio with each new set of students. I do what I ask them to do. If, in my Young Adult Literature course, I ask them to do some sort of project using literature for their classroom or library, then I do the same—a new project for each new set of students. Only then can I understand the time constraints, the computer glitches, the lines at the library, whatever. It is also important to me that I maintain a fresh approach each semester. I want to be doing something new and different so I can be looking at new books all the time. After the initial few weeks of a semester, the students are sharing artifacts they are collecting more and more and I am called upon to share less and less.

My portfolios tend to have themes because that is how I tend to organize my thoughts. However, the themes emerge late in the collection process. I'm nervous about a portfolio until that theme emerges—although I think the anguished thinking I go through to find the theme is quite worthwhile for me. Students, too, sometimes allow themes to help them see what matters, or makes sense for them. One inservice teacher shared how her life had influenced a theme she saw emerging in her portfolio. She and her husband were building a new house, and everywhere she looked she saw blueprints. Her portfolio, then, took on a blueprint format—the floors of her imaginary portfolio home. The basement is the foundation research that holds together the rest of her portfolio. It contains articles, class handouts, etc. The main floor contains her presentation of the novel reading she has done in the literature course. The top floor contains her personal writing artifacts. The theme, she said, helped her to select the artifacts that made sense for her.

Additionally, I like to share picture books that model the portfolio process. These books are hands-on examples that give a more global approach than can portfolios I have kept, or am continuing to keep. These titles allow examples from a variety of cultures, as well as different formats. My portfolios may not make sense for my students, but one of the picture book portfolio examples often will. (A list of picture books that model portfolios can be found in the "Suggested Reading" section at the end of this book.)

Occasionally, students still struggle with making the transition between what matters to me, or a picture book author, and what matters to them. I ask them to close their eyes and think of their homes. What do they see that could tell us about them? How can they represent the aspects that are a vital part of who they are and what matters to them? Often this visualization will spark the offerings of a few members of class. Their comments will often be exactly what someone struggling with the concept needs to hear. If they are still unsure, I show them my children's portfolios. The early offerings contain literacy artifacts from their bedroom walls, from the refrigerator, from areas of the house that contain their treasures. Again, this sharing lends itself to illustrating in a concrete way exactly what is important to an individual. This is especially important when explaining portfolios to small children.

Selection   I always begin my selection discussion by sharing the artifacts from one of my professional portfolios (see Figure 1–5). I compiled this specific portfolio as my doctoral comprehensive exam. The theme of the portfolio was "Valuing Diverse Voices." Each section begins with a quotation that is meaningful to me, and hopefully descriptive of the artifact.

Additionally, I help my students with the selection process by making "suggestions" (this is where we talk about euphemistic language choices) on inclusion items. I select several items they must include, as illustrated by the lists in Figure 1–6.

Finally, we share in class, always, what we are selecting for our portfolios. If I see a particular student struggling with the concept, I will help him or her as they share what they are doing in practicum, or if they are talking about a personal hobby, I point out that an artifact representing this may be useful in their portfolio. Listening is a very important part of helping students select meaningful artifacts for their porfolios—listening, not only on the part of the teacher to point them out, but also on the part of the students to see how they can make another student's choice fit their own portfolio.

Reflection   This is, no doubt, an area that is very difficult for most of my students. They struggle with writing "why" an artifact is included. Of late, we've stopped saying "why" over and over again, hoping that if we shout the word they'll understand better. Instead, we've tried to illustrate what that may mean in terms of their portfolio. We do this with an activity that has proven quite successful for us in classrooms of young children, in classrooms full of pre- and inservice teachers, and also in presentations about portfolios we do around the country.

We begin with a cookie assortment box. A candy assortment box would probably work just as well, but we like Pepperidge Farm cookies. At any rate, we talk about how Pepperidge Farm has already done the collection and selection processes on these cookies. They may have chosen the best sellers, or they may have selected those cookies that they can't move, or whatever. Our point comes in the individual cookies we will all select when asked to choose only one. After each individual has chosen a cookie, we ask them to explain *why* they picked that particular cookie. Some of the answers we have received: "I chose the Chessmen because they are different. I am one of eight kids and I always wanted to be different. I've noticed that now I may choose something just because it is the opposite of what my siblings choose, no other reason, I just want to be different." Or, "I chose the Pirouette because it is a mix of chocolate and vanilla. I don't like too much of any one flavor or taste. I like mixtures, in most things in my life. I guess you could say I'm eclectic." Or, "I waited until all the boxes of cookies had reached me. I couldn't choose until I had all my options placed in front of me. I'm afraid to make choices without careful thought and planning. I'm not a risk taker."

While this may seem a trite way to explain the reflection process, the answers others give help individuals articulate that they are different; that they make choices and selections based on something they know about themselves but have rarely given voice to. This simple exercise, the follow-up discussion, and the listening all give this thought process a concrete example to hook onto.

Projection   This is an area that we work on throughout the semester. My students and I are always sharing, always finding ways to explain what matters to us, always finding different ways to "publish" what our portfolio says about us. I hold personal conferences with students on an individual basis throughout the semester, culminating in a final tour at the end of each semester. Additionally, we all share via e-mail, letters, notes, and comments throughout the semester. Returning students often begin new courses with me by offering to share their portfolios with those students who are unfamiliar with the concept.

We offer workshops throughout the semester for graduate students working on their master's portfolios in order to share where we all are in the process. The final oral presentation is open, by invitation, to those attempting the process.

Figure 1–1: *Portfolio requirements for Reading/Language Arts Methods course*

We will be assembling portfolios for assessment purposes in this course. A portfolio reflects the person responsible for compiling it. No two portfolios will be alike, although I have certain requirements that you must all complete for inclusion in your portfolio. Other individual literacy artifacts which you choose to place in your particular portfolio will be up to you.

The following items you must include in your portfolio. You must have sections on: Myself as a Reader, Myself as a Writer, Myself as a Listener, Myself as a Speaker, Myself as a Teacher/Learner, Myself as a Monitor/Assessor, Myself as a Community Member, and Who I Am. Each section should have a reflection piece framing it as well. This reflection piece should answer the question "SO WHAT?" about the items included in the section.

Required elements for each section are as follows:

1) MYSELF AS A READER:
    *   Reaction to Required Books Read
    After reading each of the four required books, write a one-page reaction to the book including what you liked or agreed with, what you disliked or disagreed with, and/or what you learned from the book. One page for each book is plenty for this. We'll use these reactions to discuss the books.
    *   Novel Literature Guide
    The literature guide that you prepare will be done with a novel that you are using with your pen pal. A complete description and format to follow is included in your packet of handouts. You will be using part of this with your pen pals.
    *   Optional Items You Could Include in This Section:
        *   Reading Autobiography (Reflection of your own reading)
        *   Reading Record (Books you've read this semester)
        *   Other
2) MYSELF AS A WRITER:
    *   Pen Pal Letters
    You will have a 5th-grade pen pal from St. Gerald Elementary School (78th & Lakeview) and a 6th-grade pen pal from Dodge Elementary School (98th & Maple). Include in your portfolio copies of your letters and copies (or originals) of the students' letters.

- Two pieces you have written this semester from rough to final draft. These can be any genre you wish—business letters, stories, poems, etc.
- Optional Items You Could Include in This Section:
  - Writing Autobiography (Reflection of your own writing)
  - Writing Record (Items you've written this semester)

3) MYSELF AS A LISTENER:

- Written Response to One Class Discussion

After one class discussion of your choice, write your reaction and what you learned from listening to others.

- Optional Items You Could Include in This Section:
  - Listening Autobiography (Reflection of your own listening)
  - Listening Journal (What you remember hearing in a day, week, etc., and the impact it had on you)
  - Other

4) MYSELF AS A SPEAKER:

- Demonstration or Storytelling

Everyone will be telling a story with some sort of props or demonstrating a hobby or some other skill with some sort of props. Examples will be done for you in class. Each person will also provide a copy of a story outline or demonstration handout for each class member. More information and examples will be given in class.

- Optional Items You Could Include in This Section:
  - Speaking Autobiography (Reflection of your own speaking)
  - Slang Journal (Slang words you have heard or used)
  - Other

5) MYSELF AS A TEACHER/LEARNER:

- Mysteries Mini-Integrated Web

You will be expected to prepare an integrated language arts mini-web or unit on mysteries. The web will have a minimum of 3 hubs or subtopics with at least 3 complete examples of language arts-related activities (reading, writing, listening, and speaking) per hub. Although you may use published materials to help you think of ideas, please retype any ideas used in your own words (in other words, don't just Xerox pages from an already prepared web—I expect you to put some thought into this). The web will also include at least 10 related children's books (published since 1980) within the web. (Do not include Golden Books, Berenstein bear books, Disney books, Care Bear books, Sesame Street books, books made from TV shows or movies, etc.—please choose *quality* children's books.) Also, find at least one poem that fits into your web and include it in your materials. An example of a web and further directions will be forthcoming.

- Teaching Philosophy

Why do you want to be a teacher? What kind of teacher would you like to be? What will be important to you as a teacher? Write a brief paper describing your teaching philosphy.

- Optional Items You Could Include in This Section:
    - Anything you prepared for use with the St. Gerald/Dodge students
    - Other

6) MYSELF AS A MONITOR/ASSESSOR:

- Reflections of Work with St. Gerald and Dodge Students

After each session with the 5th- and 6th-grade students, write a brief description of what happened and your assessment of the student you are working with.

- Self-Assessment

You will have input on your own grade for this class. In your self-assessment, tell me the grade you think you have earned in this class. Consider the quality of your work and other matters, such as professionalism. Professionalism means that you come to class and participate in the class activities and discussions. I expect you to attend all class sessions. In the event of bad weather, please call me to find out if we are having class.

7) MYSELF AS COMMUNITY MEMBER:

- What I Learned From Being a Part of a Community of Learners

Write a short paper on what you learned from the other students in this class or the elementary students you worked with.

8) WHO I AM:

- What Is Important to Me

This could be done in many ways—through photographs, narrative, or even a list of things/people that are important to you. What is important to us is all part of who we are as teachers and learners. Explore that in this section.

Figure 1–2: Items to include in a portfolio

Some possible elements for reading and writing portfolios:

- Favorite poems and songs
- Articles from newspapers, magazines, and journals that encourage thoughts regarding reading, writing, or teaching
- Finished writing samples that might include:
    persuasive writing
    letter writing
    poetry
    informative writing
    stories
- Writing across the curriculum that might include:
    reports
    journals
    literature logs
- Literature extensions that might include:
    drama script
    puppets
    webs
    pocket chart cards or ideas
    other extension ideas
- Record of books read and books to be read in the future
- Writing responses to literary components that might include:
    plot
    setting
    point of view
    character development
    links to life
    theme
    literary links
- Writing that illustrates critical thinking about readings
- Notes from individual reading and writing conferences
- Writing that shows growth in usage of traits:
    growing ability in self-correction
    punctuation

> spelling
>
> grammar
>
> handwriting legibility

- Samples in which ideas are changed from first to final draft
- Unedited first draft
- Revised final draft
- Writing that illustrates evidence of topic generation
- Self-assessment
- Photos of readers, writers, or learners
- Information about yourself that informs your reading, writing, or learning
- Other:

_____

Figure 1–3: *Grading rubric for portfolio*

An "A" portfolio includes assignments and other pieces that:

- Clearly convey an understanding of the topic.
- Contain appropriate activities for children.
- Demonstrate evidence of critical thought and problem solving.
- Show evidence of productive reflection.
- Use reading and writing to satisfy various goals.
- Show evidence of being a lifelong reader/writer.
- Are of professional quality in terms of the mechanics and conventions of writing (few if any typos, misspellings, usage errors, etc.).
- Self-assessment not only tells what is in the portfolio, but also is reflective of learning and yourself as a reader/writer. Absences from class are few and are explained.

A "B" portfolio includes assignments and other pieces that:

- Convey a surface understanding of the topic.
- Contain some questionable activities for children.
- Demonstrate evidence of presenting information in an academic way only with no critical thought or reflection.
- Use reading and writing to meet others' goals only.
- Show some indication of being a lifelong reader/writer.
- Lack some professional quality in terms of the mechanics and conventions of writing (some typos, misspellings, usage errors, etc.).
- Self-assessment explains what is in the portfolio, but lacks reflection of learning. More absences and lack of explanation.

A "C" portfolio includes assignments and other pieces that:

- Do not convey a clear understanding of the topic.
- Lack appropriate activities for children.
- Are missing assignments or elements of assignments.
- Are apathetic or resistant to reading/writing.
- Show little or no indication of being a lifelong reader/writer.
- Show poor quality of writing in terms of mechanics (many typos, misspellings, usage errors, etc.).

- Self-assessment contains surface comments only or is missing. Numerous absences from class with no explanation.

A "D" or "F" portfolio includes assignments and other pieces that:

- Do not show understanding of topic.
- Lack appropriate activities for children.
- Are missing several assignments or elements of assignments.
- Are apathetic or resistant to reading/writing.
- Show no indication of being a lifelong reader/writer.
- Show very poor quality of writing in terms of mechanics.
- Self-assessment not evident. A substantial number of classes missed with no explanation.

Figure 1–4: Portfolio conference questions/prompts

1. Tell me about what you learned from keeping a portfolio.
2. What is the most important or most meaningful piece in your portfolio? Why?
3. What is the least important or least meaningful piece in your portfolio? Why?
4. How would you describe yourself as a reader or writer (or learner in general)?
5. What is your philosophy of teaching reading/language arts?
6. Other comments.
7. Grade discussion.
8. Where do you go from here? What are you writing next? What are you reading next? What are your lingering questions?

Figure 1–5: Sample artifact

> In daily conversation, ideas are mixed with anecdotes and jokes, humor stands cheek-by-jowl with tragedy, business with non-sense, anger with love. Increasingly I see life here as these word-snapshots strung together in an ill-kept photo album . . . The fabric of the . . . community is not the empty spaces in the album, but rather the photographs wherever we find them scattered throughout the pages. During the quiet times . . . when it seems that nothing is going on, there is for the people here a continuing appreciation for the last vignette, an anticipation of the next. Indeed, the echoes and resonances are often even more satisfying than the events themselves. (Welsch 1990, xviii)

This quotation serves as an introduction to this portfolio. It is a collection of "snapshots strung together"—these are the artifacts. This portfolio is also the "echoes and resonances" of those snapshots or events—these are the reflection pieces explaining the inclusions.

I've been asked why I wanted to do a portfolio and I keep coming back to the same answer: because it makes sense for me. I repeatedly beg my students to ask that question of themselves—"Does this make sense?" I believe I must, in effect, practice what I preach. Mem Fox (1993, 2) sums it up better than I can. She writes: "I like doing this because it matters." Well, I didn't always like preparing my portfolio. It has been a painful process at times, sometimes I just wanted to sleep, but I kept at it because it matters, to me.

I learned a great deal from this experience. If for no other reason, it helped me to think about the voices that have been influential in my doctoral program. Most of all, it has caused me to think. I know it would have been easier to lock myself in a room and write for several days: I can do that. I've learned to "student," but it wouldn't have been as meaningful for me.

The process of developing this portfolio has taken over a year. I've stacked items that I thought might make sense to include. I've thought about what I believe. I've read and written and listened and discussed and then did them all again. During the first year, I've realized I am a social-constructivist; I had previously described myself as a naturalist, or a whole language teacher. I've discovered that although I have firm beliefs and the research to support them, I still find it most valuable to listen to other views. I can learn from anything, which reminds me of a hopefully illustrative story. I was in labor with my first child, nine long years ago. I was not having a good time. During that mind-bending agony, I realized I would finally be able to understand all those labor stories my aunts and mother would share. I was about to become a "member of the club." I try to keep that incident in mind while I continue on this journey. Pain, insult, loneliness, defeat, failure, success, hopefulness, joy—all can teach. I try to learn from everything because I enjoy the feeling of learning.

I've learned that I have a valuable voice, and this may have been, for me, the most difficult lesson. I am my own worst enemy, and as Sally Kempton wrote, "it is hard to fight an enemy who has outposts in your head." But, I have come to realize as I watch the respondent in my dissertation study, valuing oneself is also modeled, or not. I must be able to afford myself, and what I have to say, as much respect as I give others.

I've listened well, but it is not finished. This is only the first vignette in a much longer story. The portfolio you view today is already out of date. It will continue to grow and change as I do. And, that is exactly what it should do, because I have not, by any measure, stopped listening.

Reflection One:

> What do I want for my students? I want them to leave my classroom knowing they are readers and writers, wanting to learn more, and having a number of strategies for that learning in any field. I want them to like learning and to like themselves. I want them to know they have important things to say and unique ways of saying them. I want them to know their voices are valued. I want learning to be fun. Most importantly, I want them to gain independence as learners, knowing and trusting their own choices. (Rief 1992, 4)

I included the following artifact because it set the theme of this portfolio—valuing diverse voices. As I look back on my graduate studies, I remember a comment I made to my brother who asked if I thought I could handle all that graduate work would ask of me. I naively answered that reading and studying were what I did anyway, that, to me, being a good English teacher was about reading and staying current. I say, naively, because I didn't know how intently I would have to listen to voices that have become vital to me, voices whose stories I am just beginning to understand.

I remember when I first started teaching I was most concerned about my students' asking me a question I didn't know the answer to. I worked hard to have all the answers, even if that sometimes meant I didn't hear the questions. I wasn't listening very well. It didn't take long for me to begin questioning a few things myself, and to begin to hear a voice in my own head. This was a voice I had heard only faintly when I student-taught grammar at a local high school. The voice asked, "Why are you doing this?" I ignored it through that experience, but as I really saw my students, and gained some confidence in myself, I realized that the voice definitely had a point. I started to turn up the volume on that voice. I started to listen to myself.

Other voices have emerged as powerful and meaningful to me over the last several years. I'm certain as I try to list them that I have neglected some, but many of those listed are voices that will continue to speak to me, for, although this is something of a summative work, it is also just the beginning.

Artifact One:

A student told me a story of a professor who had really impressed her with his knowledge of a specific subject area. She was amazed at all the professor knew. Actually, she said it had left her feeling a little inadequate and small. She added, "But you're different than that, Sheri." (Now I was the one feeling inadequate and small.) But she didn't stop there. She added, "You're impressed with what I know. You're impressed with what I have to say—you take notes on what we say! You're impressed with what we can do. That feels wonderful because I've started to believe you might be right."

My students may forget what I say, they may sell their textbooks the minute the semester ends, they may never remember the name of the countless books I read to them, but they'll NEVER forget the way I make them feel. I hope they leave my class feeling valued and capable and impressed with what they can do. For like Rief, "I want them to know their voices are valued." (1992, 4)

Figure 1–6: Portfolio requirements and suggestions

Course Requirements:

We will be assembling portfolios for assessment purposes in this course. A portfolio authentically reflects the learner responsible for compiling it. No two portfolios are alike. Each portfolio should represent the individual who keeps it. The individual artifacts you choose will be up to you, with the exception of those artifacts listed under "my suggestions"—those are required. The items you choose may include, but are not limited to, the following:

- book lists
- favorite poems, songs, letters, quotations
- projects, surveys, reports, and/or units
- interesting thoughts
- finished writing—a variety of genres
- literature logs
- videotape of reading/teaching
- literature extension activities
- audiotapes of reading/teaching
- writing responses to literary components (plot, setting, point of view, character development, links to life, theme, literary links and criticism)
- writing that illustrates critical thinking and readings
- notes from individual reading and writing conferences
- samples in which ideas are modified from first draft to final project
- self-evaluations
- journal writing
- literary artifacts from your past and/or present

My "Suggestions" for Our Portfolios:

A. A personal teaching philosophy. Sheri will provide an example of her current teaching philosophy.
B. Each individual will be responsible for "keeping" class minutes for a session of class. Additionally, each individual must bring copies for the other members of the class the following week. Again, Sheri will provide an example.
C. We will be visiting a junior high and a high school to practice our ideas on real students. This practicum time must be documented in the form of lesson plans and an analysis of each event. Sheri will provide an example.

An artifact representing each of the following sections must also be included in the portfolio:

"I am a reader."

"I am a writer."

"I am a family member."

"I am a member of a learning community."

"I am a self-assessor."

"I am a listener."

"I am a speaker."

"I am a learner/teacher."

2 | Tour of the Portfolio

Learning to listen to myself required action: I asked ill-formed questions, practiced, formulated more questions, read and practiced some more. I became more aware of what worked and didn't work for me. . . . Donald Graves

Developing a listening voice, that sense of self that says "that's where they are; here's where I am," starts as soon as I read something new or listen to another person speak about her writing. If this voice is tentative in its judgments, it is audacious in its questions, constantly seeking to formulate further questions that will embrace a subject, however elusive it seems. The new voice demands facts. For the learner, shifts in voice are evidence of growth. They say, "Aha, I'm on the right track to . . . a whole new idea, a whole new way of looking at things." Donald Graves

This chapter includes introduction pieces students have used to frame their portfolios. Each introduction reflects the personality of the individual who owns the portfolio. No two introductions are the same, just as no two portfolios, or people, are the same.

The artifacts selected were chosen because they illustrate the choices made by a variety of preservice and inservice teachers. All reflect the personalities of the individuals depicted.

❚ This poem introduced a portfolio from a young woman whose previous portfolio had been stolen. She wrote this poem to any potential future thieves who might rob her of what she holds dear. She wrote this particular poem as an opening piece to her second portfolio, in Sheri's linguistics course, where she was an undergraduate one course shy of student teaching. Her introduction not only sets the tone for the rest of the portfolio, but it allows a glimpse of just how vital this portfolio is to the individual who keeps it.

Dear Occupant of My Portfolio:

This leather binder you hold in your hand
is more than just a leather case.
It may hold no relevance for you
other than the leather's value,
But let me warn you, Reader,
its contents are priceless.

Within this $50 case
exists hard work and knowledge
Which may hold no meaning to you
other than the cash fact.
But let me tell to you, Reader,
the lessons learned were invaluable.

And if you should come upon my portfolio, Reader,
with intentions less than honorable,
Please take it.
You obviously need it more than I.

You see, Dear Occupant of My Portfolio,
you can never steal the thoughts
stored on my worthless, dollar disk,
And those are worth a million.

Owner of This Portfolio ❚

❚ This particular student was a nontraditional undergraduate student in English/language arts secondary methods. She was a single mother who had learned a great deal from her two sons, as is evidenced by the fact that several of the topics and areas of interest dealt specifically with what listening to them, as well as to music, had taught her.

This student understood that Gardner's Seven Intelligences (Logical/Mathematical, Linguistic, Spatial, Interpersonal, Intrapersonal, Kinesthetic, and Musical) could certainly be emphasized and valued in a portfolio format. Her musical intelligence taught her that particular songs had illustrated vivid connections.

These so-called multiple intelligences are a useful and meaningful starting place for individuals beginning a portfolio. Asking how one illuminates her "spatial intelligence," for example, might be a way to expand the portfolio possibilities.

I chose song lyrics as the theme for my portfolio because I believe that they remind us that we're not the only one who has ever felt a certain way. We can find parts of ourselves and our experiences in song lyrics. This is important for students (young people) who often feel they are alone in the world.

Contents

Dance ballerina dance

Life's a dance

Slightly off key

Step by step

Melody

Lyrics make the meaning

Twist & Shout

Unchained Melody

Trip the light fantastic

Footloose

One step forward, two steps back

A Song in my heart

Music to my ears

Dance to a different drummer

Dance to the light of the moon

Sound of music

Sheri's suggestions

My sons

Misc. personal pieces

Misc. lesson plans

Articles on writing

Poetry suggestions

Misc. language articles

Articles on portfolios

Bulletin board ideas

Student Life

Vocabulary

My writing

Sheri's gifts

Book talks

Class minutes/methods

6th grade writers ▮

▮ This first-year teacher decided to turn her portfolio into a Dr. Seuss book of sorts. She used the format of Dr. Seuss' rhyming books to describe and reflect upon what was in her portfolio. She also talked about the importance of teacher modeling as she took the reader on a journey through her portfolio. She does practice what she teaches with her students, modeling her own learning as she works with children.

Congratulations!
Today is your day.
You're off to see
what a superior portfolio can be.

Things you will see:
- Dedication
- Language Arts Requirements
- Life Long Writing
- Harrison School Writing
- My Students
- Personal Inspirations

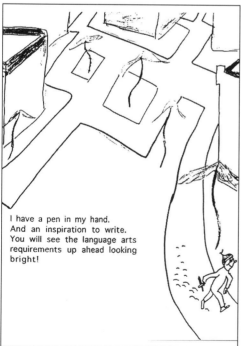

I have a pen in my hand.
And an inspiration to write.
You will see the language arts
requirements up ahead looking
bright!

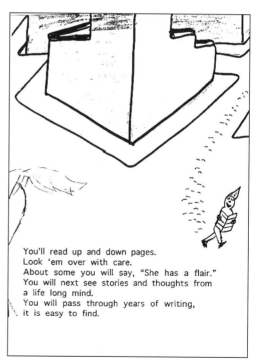

You'll read up and down pages.
Look 'em over with care.
About some you will say, "She has a flair."
You will next see stories and thoughts from
a life long mind.
You will pass through years of writing,
it is easy to find.

Out here things can happen, and frequently do.
My fifth graders are clever and creative too!
You will find writings for school and parents galore.
After seeing how these students are, you will be yelling for more!

You'll be on your way up!
To a very favorite spot,
My personal favorites,
I think they're quite hot!

You will see things about me
and why I love to teach.
Like the old saying goes,
"Practice what you preach."

I hope you have enjoyed this trip through me. I know that there was a lot to see.

So...
be your name Rufus or Maxy or Billoby Ray, "I must create a portfolio too," you all will say.

So please start now, your paper is waiting. It will be too much fun creating.

❙ This individual was a graduate student in adolescent literature. She was a former teacher working in the media center of the district offices and quite interested in building her expertise in several arenas. She was very organized and saw fit not only to organize her portfolio with a table of contents, but also to differentiate materials among her notebook, a three-ring binder, and her file cabinet, which held more detailed articles and works.

Portfolio
Table of Contents

Notebook

Section 1: Class notes

Section 2: Projects

Section 3: Reading list

Files

File 1: Reflection & Information Data Sheet (with photo)

File 2: Class handouts

File 3: Class handouts (with annotations & photo)

File 4: Bibliographies & Literature Reviews (with annotations)

File 5: Censorship Articles (with annotations)

File 6: General Interest Articles (includes annotated articles on portfolio assessment, multicultural literature & selection)

File 7: Mystery Unit

File 8: Unit Background Materials ❙

❙ This middle school home economics teacher was enrolled in a graduate language arts class (TED 8470, hence the case #8470). She saw the connections that reading, writing, listening, and speaking had for her content area. Her portfolio took the form of a crime scene, with her artifacts appearing as exhibits in the case. Her creative nature found its way throughout her portfolio, as you are about to see.

Case #8470
Suspect: Alisa
Alias: Ms. Hoffman
Investigator: Detective K. Danielson

Crime: Alisa has been charged of the following literary felony charges:

- Willfully displaying an understanding of literature topics
- Designing and implementing creative and appropriate literature activities in her classroom to achieve various goals
- Suspected of using her critical thinking and problem-solving skills

- She has been caught "read" handed reading books in her free time
- Alisa also has a record of attending language arts classes every Wednesday night this past semester

Prosecution Exhibit A:
Professional Reading Responses

Alisa has clearly shown an unlawful interest in professional readings such as: *Build a Literate Classroom* by Donald Graves, *Radical Reflections* by Mem Fox, and various articles in professional journals. Alisa's critical thought and reflection to these professional readings will give you some insight into how her criminal mind works.

Alisa has not had a criminal past in literature but her attendance at a late night class with other literature outlaws has corrupted her. Ms. Hoffman has actually been thinking about how she can incorporate reading and writing into her curriculum, but now she is making a conscious effort to corrupt her own students into having a passion for reading and writing.

Prosecution Exhibit B:
Work Submitted For Publication

Ms. Hoffman's devious works have been part of a publication in the world-renowned Omaha World Herald. Ms. Hoffman and her classes submitted responses to the Omaha World Herald's survey question, "What skills do you need to acquire before leaving home?" Each of the students wrote a response to the Omaha World Herald along with Ms. Hoffman. As you can clearly see, Alisa has also begun to corrupt the youth of Omaha into reading and writing.

Although Ms. Hoffman's response did not get published, one of her students, Dawni, did get her response published. Ms. Hoffman's work was too amusing for the conservative paper to publish, but you will find her work attached to the prosecution exhibit.

Prosecution Exhibit C:
Subject Mapping—Food and Nutrition

This evidence pretty much explains itself. Ms. Hoffman has taken her Food and Nutrition unit and has incorporated an absurd amount of reading and writing activities into the curriculum. The activities are appropriate for many ages. These activities clearly prove that Ms. Hoffman has an understanding of literature and has intentionally developed lessons that students will enjoy and that will encourage them to read and write.

The Food and Nutrition web consists of five major areas: Multicultural Aspects of Food, the Food Pyramid, Fruits, Vegetables, and Children's Cooking. Each of the areas incorporate activities for students of all ages. Many of the ideas from the fruit and vegetable sections were influenced by a CD-ROM program produced by the Dole Fruit Company. Although some of the ideas came from the program, many of the activities were Ms. Hoffman's original ideas. (The Dole Company is also under investigation for corrupting the minds of our youth.)

Along with the food web, you will find a list of activities and literature that Ms. Hoffman incorporates into her quarter Family and Consumer Science course. This list is not in its entirety; as we were collecting evidence from Ms. Hoffman's plan book we found that several papers had been shredded. We suspect that she has other incriminating evidence in those lesson plans as well.

Suspect's Testimony: Alisa
December 7, 1994

I, Alisa Jo Hoffman, of sound mind and body, do hereby testify that I am guilty of the charges brought against me.

- I have clearly conveyed an understanding of the literature topics discussed in this course.
- I have knowingly and willfully designed appropriate activities for my students.
- I have demonstrated critical thought, reflection, and problem solving.
- I have used reading and writing to satisfy various goals in my professional and personal life.
- I enjoy curling up with a good book in my spare time.
- I have attended class every Wednesday this semester.

In this case I plead guilty and ask those prosecuting me to have mercy upon my soul. ▌

3 | I Am a Collector

Students put all kinds of work into their portfolios that they see as important to them as learners. Teachers do the same. As a result, students are drawing a much better profile of themselves as learners. They now connect literacy with their everyday living—in school and out.   Donald Graves

Artifacts in this chapter show that students are unique in what they collect or notice, in school and out of school. Portfolios allow for this. They provide the individual with a medium to help make the walls between school and home invisible. As Graves indicates, our literate lives should not end at the threshold of the school; our literate lives must permeate our very existence.

The collector in us allows for connections between and among our literate lives. What we collect and how we view these collections are yet another demonstration of our literate connections. Some students collect quotes, some collect interesting words or poems. The collection is not nearly as vital as the link it exhibits: students view their literate selves beyond the classroom. Their search for literate meaning in their everyday lives is at the heart of the concept of student as collector. A portfolio allows students to show that side of their literacy as well, and values the collective nature of teachers and learners.

The following artifacts represent connections students are making throughout their lives in their portfolios. They find artifacts that "speak" to them, but perhaps a category is not immediately evident to them. These artifacts may, indeed, serve as writing ideas, or perhaps they will serve as artifacts to share with students in the form of "something I came across in the paper today that caught my eye. What do you think of it?" Perhaps the collection aspect of a portfolio has not been extended much beyond that point. It is a hodgepodge of items of interest. But more than anything else, it serves to illustrate how the process of collecting meaningful items has pervaded the students' very being. They look for things that matter to them. The process may not have been totally completed, but it is the process it represents that makes those artifacts meaningful. Sometimes this is the first step for those students who are struggling with the concept of a portfolio. "I found this cartoon about literacy and I want to keep it somewhere so I won't lose it."

The artifact itself is not as vital as the process it represents. Merely the modeling with students of being fascinated by articles, cartoons, or photographs serves to illustrate the connection between school and outside the school. It allows for students to do the same, to bring to the classroom those things that they are wondering about, questioning, and are fascinated by. Especially in terms of language interest, this is vital to students' gaining a "richer interconnection of parts" (Smith 1985, 163).

▌ This undergraduate student collected quotes in a special notebook. As he notes in his reflection, he is selective about this collection. He doesn't write down just any quote. The quote has to make him pause and think before it makes it into his notebook. The selection process makes him a critical listener and reader. Both are important processes to model for his own students eventually.

Some people collect coins, stamps, or dolls. I collect quotes.

I started my collection when I was a freshman in college and have been adding to it ever since.

I only include quotes that I find important. They have come from a variety of places: books, magazines, teachers, friends, movies—just about everywhere.

Very few are what you would call "famous quotes by famous people." If I see something that strikes me, I put it in my special spiral and it becomes part of me. I am very selective about what is good enough to be put in the special notebook. Only about one in five quotes that are good enough to make me pause are good enough to make it.

I have included a sample of what is in my special spiral of quotes.

If a doctor, lawyer, or
dentist has 40 people in his
office at one time,
all of whom had different needs,
and some of whom didn't want
to be there and were causing trouble,
and the doctor, lawyer, or dentist,
without assistance,
had to treat them all with
professional excellence for nine months,
then he might have some conception of the
classroom teacher's job.
Donald O. Quinn

- Make a true estimate of your own ability then raise it 10 percent.
- The relaxed person is the powerful person.
- Always be on the lookout for the big idea that can change your life.
- Nature siphons off boredom. ▌

▌ This artifact and reflection are from the portfolio of a student in Teaching English Linguistically, an undergraduate course for secondary majors. The particular student represented here was asked to find and discover language around her that she found interesting and compelling. I have a list of my favorite words and I share it with students, illustrating how I sometimes use the words when I need a place to go for my poetry.

In linguistics we revel in the sound of words, rolling them around on our tongues, discussing the marvelous feel and sound of some of our favorites. Many of my students are amazed that other people have favorite words—evidently the subject of words has never come up in seventeen years of English classes!

The artifact and reflection illustrate how excited students can become about the tools of our literacy trade: *words*.

WWWWWOOOOORRRRRDDDDDSSSSS

As always an important part of language is the words which make up a particular language. Words are fun. They mean different things to different people, and many times words can be used to enhance a given conversation or story. Words are unique because they have so much power. Words can hurt or heal. Words can cause a fight or be used to set things right. Words can teach. Words can tell. Words can make sense, or make fun. Words can express love, hate, sympathy, or concern . . . words are everything and everywhere. Words are language.

I love to look at words and read them. Some are so melodic! Others are dry and boring. But most important, words are a serious matter. Anything with so much power is serious. Therefore, choose your words carefully so nobody gets hurt.

In this section of my portfolio I include artifacts which are made up of words. What I mean is that most of these artifacts are unique because they are made up of words. Someone took words and formed something special from them. For example, the song "Storybook Love" by Willy DeVille contains beautiful words which were put together to form an incredible love song. I have included the following page of words, which are some of my favorites. Some are real, some are sort of made up, some have an explanation, others don't.

So, READ on!

```
        fluid          sweet           sculpture

     however;          care            pursed

 care     vibrate      lover      rapidly      how rude!

    imagination     embracing    serenity    positively

picaterian:  someone who is not picky or particular (courtesy of
             my co-worker, Trudy)

    scrambled      illusion     dilemma        defiance

       miracle     curiously       animosity


STUD MUFFIN:  a term used to describe my brother Frank after his
             miraculous transformation by his wife, Betsy


  contemptuously         monocercous        jabber    bolgna

      icon       flowing        haughty      trepidation

  hastifolious    reveling    pillow    fracture    female

  wrenched      friends     gentleman    crafty     ensued

  special      together      furious    vaguely     twinkle

    salty      recolonization         denuded        home

 agitation   honesty        family             tranquility

      love          hope          joy      ideal

         serenity     captivating

NERTZ:  as opposed to shit

Booking:  a term used to explain how we put jewelry into
          inventory books

DUH:  a word used to describe a customer when they come in and
      ask something stupid
```

▌This artifact and reflection were provided by a nontraditional undergraduate student in secondary English/language arts methods. She had learned from her experience as a single mom of two boys that the process was as important as the product. This is evidenced by the reflection and the artifact that follows. Most exciting about this artifact is that the student sees literacy in her everyday life. She has learned to value her personal experiences for what they have taught her, and the way in which literacy connects with her real life is also evident here.

I included this artifact because it illustrates how my search for meaning has pervaded even my music listening time. These words, particularly meaningful to me, are from a John Michael Montgomery song. I think this song applies to my personal philosophy of teaching: we learn from doing, to paraphrase Frank Smith.

Even listening to music can be about "feeding" my portfolio. I look for things to add everywhere. The collection aspect of the portfolio process is very clear and important to me.

> Life's a dance you learn as you go,
>> sometimes you lead,
>> sometimes you follow.
> Don't worry about what you don't know,
> Life's a dance you learn as you go. ▌

4

I Am a Reader

A *lifelong literate person chooses books independently and reads them without undue prodding.*   Donald Graves

If you are not a reader of a wide variety of material from the present and the past, how will you know what to write about or how to write effectively? If you are not a reader, how will you know the books that children might love?

Mem Fox

Teachers of readers must be readers themselves. Not only readers, but enthusiastic readers. If you don't have it, you can't pass it on.

In our classes, students are given time to read for pleasure. Many schools have cute acronyms for this: BEAR (Be Excited About Reading), DEAR (Drop Everything and Read), SSR (Sustained Silent Reading), SQUIRT (Super Quiet Uninterrupted Reading Time), etc. What it's called isn't important. What is important is that students are given time and choice in their reading.

We are known in our building as "the cart ladies," because we both take an enormous rolling cart of books with us to every class we teach. We begin each session with Sustained Silent Reading. The cart provides books for those students who need a new one. Following Sustained Silent Reading, we share what books we are currently reading or are excited about. At the beginning of the semester we are usually the ones who share our reading with the class. But soon, students see this as not only an opportunity to share their enthusiasm, but also a great chance to hear from their peers about other good books to read.

In a content-area reading course in which students are asked to read at least one book for pleasure, numerous preservice teachers share that they haven't read a book for pleasure since junior high. Many of them think pleasure reading is an oxymoron. However, it doesn't take long for them to remember what they enjoyed about reading. And the invitation to read for pleasure allows them the freedom to do so, opening the door once again into the "literacy club."

The following artifacts represent how our preservice and inservice teachers see themselves as readers. The way they represent this tells more than what they read. It serves to illustrate the literate beings they have rediscovered.

▌This first-year teacher is a reader. Although her district requires her to use a basal, she does so sparingly. She has used novel units with her students and encourages them to read books of their own choosing, too. In her response to the book *Radical Reflections* by Mem Fox, she addresses her own beliefs about reading and her own reading practices.

So why read? J. E. Dinger once wrote, "Do not mistake acquirement of mere knowledge for power. Like food, these things must be digested and assimilated to become life or force. Learning is not wisdom; knowledge is not necessarily vital energy. The student who has to cram through a school or college course, who has made himself merely a receptacle for the teacher's thoughts and ideas, is not educated; he has not gained much. He is a reservoir, not a fountain. One retains, the other gives forth. Unless his knowledge is converted into wisdom, into faculty, it will become stagnant like still water."

As a teacher, it is most important to be like a fountain always giving forth. This is done through a constant thirst for knowledge that can be satiated through books. This also serves as a needed role model for the classroom. I, as the teacher, read and learn along with my students, thus promoting the importance of lifelong learning. The teacher who does not read and expand his or her micro-self will fall into a rut where he or she will remain, like stagnant water. I read to expand myself and my interests. My goal is to be as well-rounded as possible in life. One of the ways to meet this goal is through reading.

Mem Fox Reaction

I thoroughly enjoyed Mem's *Radical Reflections*. I found her book to be very comforting to read at the time because I was struggling with the writing process in my classroom. Since I did not have books until the seventh week of school, I turned to a writers' workshop for reading/language time. I was finding myself frustrated when I always had pushed certain students along to get them to write. Mem made me look closer and re-evaluate what I was doing for those students.

I felt touched by Mem when she expressed that she writes to touch the hearts of her readers. I could not agree more. (It is nice to know that someone is interested in doing the thing you are trying to do.) I think that it is crucial for authors to consider their audiences and their impacts when they write. I like how she expressed "real language" equaled "real meaning" for her readers. This makes her books much more enjoyable for readers, no matter what age, gender, or race.

I thought her book was very interesting because of the many facets included. It has sections of poetry, dialogues, opinionated insights, and important advice for the beginning teacher.

I was stunned when I read the section on basals. I could not agree more. I have always been told students learn through teacher modeling. I see proof of this every day in my classroom. It is hard for me to model the joys that I experience in reading when I do not sit down and read a basal in my free time. I read books. The world does not open up to you through a basal reader, but it can through books. I set up novel units in my class, and it was amazing how motivated my students were to read than when they read from their basals. I know we are required to teach from the basals, and I do when I have to, but I find reading to be much more involved and enjoyable when I can teach from a book. My students are very low in their reading abilities according to C.A.T. scores, but there is a desire to read when there is an actual book in their hand. It also gives them a feeiing of accomplishment when they finish those books, and are able to discuss and react to them as the intelligent sixth graders I know them to be. I think that Mem brought up some wonderful and very powerful points not only with what basals do not expose our students to, but also how they treat our students. My students are intelligent enough to read from a book, not just a modification of one. ∎

▌This middle school teacher read the book *Harris and Me* by Gary Paulsen. She also read it aloud to her own students. She was asked to keep a response journal and develop some activities with the book. Then she met with other teachers who had read the book to discuss it and their ideas. This student was the only one in her group who really liked the book. The other teachers mentioned that they weren't sure it was appropriate for children. This teacher begged to differ, which she does in her reflection piece. The book also was bittersweet for this teacher because it took place on a farm. She had recently lost her grandmother and had reflected on life on her grandparents' farm, much like the setting of this book. She felt a personal connection to the book because of her life experiences. All of these points she makes in her own reflection on the artifact.

Response Log and Literature Guide
This section shows my ideas to promote the book Harris and Me.
   "So what?"
   With my grandmother's death last week, I had the chance to go back to where she and my grandfather lived. They had a fantastic farm. When I was there, I thought of this book and had a completely new set of reactions. I wish there was time to go back and add to my reactions. When I left the farm on Saturday, I felt a little like "Me" in the book. I knew that that place had touched my life and that it would never be the same again. I pray I never forget what it was like to be on that farm.
   A few class meetings ago, we got together with the other members of the class who read the same book that we chose. That discussion was very interesting to me. The other people who read this book didn't care for it at all. They thought it taught many inappropriate lessons and bordered on desperate attempts to entertain. I got the feeling that they would rather not promote the book. I had quite the opposite reaction to the book. I've never laughed so hard while reading a book. I couldn't tell enough people about it. I wonder if our differences in opinion could be age related, because my group members were a generation ahead of me. I don't think this book is any different than any television show that is on now. People attempting to kill others on television is worse than jumping on a horse's back and a few swear words here and there. I realize that some of the events in the story should not be tried at home, but it is no worse than television. Maybe, as a teacher, I need to show a disclaimer on the board before I begin reading. What is the one? "These are trained professionals. Do not attempt this at your own home."
   This log and guide have open-ended questions and activities for real purposes. I enjoyed putting them together. I also have a large list of companion books that would go great with this story.

Response Log and Literature Guide

Book: Paulsen, G. 1993. *Harris and Me*. San Diego: Harcourt Brace & Company.

Personal Response

Chapter 1:   I found myself wondering what happened to make "Me" move around so much. I know that his parents were unable to take care of him, but shouldn't he have been able to stay in one place? I wonder if "Me" felt a culture shock when he was riding in the car with the sheriff to the Larson's place. Or when he arrived at their home. And what a first impression Harris makes! I couldn't believe that an author could come up with a boy like Harris. I had never read this book before, and decide to read it out loud to my 6th graders. I did change the swear words, but I didn't tell the kids that. They fell in love with the book, and Harris, right away.

Chapter 2:   I would've loved to see a meal at the Larson house. Louie eating everything first, without chewing. Knute sitting, silent, drinking coffee with both hands. The ladies in the kitchen and the boys fighting for food. All before the sun is even thinking about rising! Nine-year-old Harris knows how to roll and smoke a cigarette? That to me is scary, but I suppose back then and being on the farm had something to do with that. Of course, "Me's" first experience with a cigarette wasn't very successful! Then "Me" has a run-in with Vivian. I laughed with my students out loud!

Chapter 3:   I loved the beginning of this chapter! With "Me" going through the "groin" pains and Harris getting smacked, I could barely read to my kids. We were wondering who Harris was wrestling with, and when we found out that it was a Rooster, we were very surprised. Harris seems able to manipulate people and situations. Poor "Me" had to do most of the cranking on the milk separator, thanks to Harris. What a kid...

Chapter 4:   The most entertaining chapter yet. I'm so surprised at this book! It makes me wonder how many other books are out there that are this crazy and fun to read. Is it the author? Or can other authors write in this fashion? I do question the swearing. But it is part of life, Harris' life, and that would probably be exactly how he would be if you could meet him in real life.

Chapter 5:   Gary Paulsen does a great job of putting the story into your head. This book is so easy to visualize. It's like a movie going on inside of you. His descriptions are very detailed. In this chapter, he lets us know just how big the horses are. And then there's Buzzer. My class and I were thinking that he was just a normal cat. Maybe the author was exaggerating when he described him as big as a collie, with a spotted coat, who had killed a dog. We would come to find out that we were really wrong!

Chapter 6:   In this chapter, we find out that Louie isn't 100% crazy after all. Harris showed "Me" the figures that Louie had carved from the wood. He had used the mice fur to make coats and clothing for the figures. Soon after that, Harris had the "Tarzan" idea. Swinging from the barn to another farm building seemed easy to Harris. This series of events made me remember my Grandpa's farm and huge barn that he had. I couldn't imagine doing the "Tarzan of the Apes" swing from Grandpa's barn. If I didn't die on the swing, I surely would've been killed by my parents!

Chapter 7:   My brother and I would play Cowboys and Indians at my grandpa's too. We would throw dirt clods instead of having knives, bows and arrows like Harris did. When Harris hit Buzzer, I though he was a dead man. Another thing I can identify with is the excitement of going to town, and most of all ORANGE POP! Grandpa and Grandma always had orange pop when we'd visit. However, we wouldn't watch Gene Autry movies.

Chapter 8:   I would think that "Me" would know by now, not to get involved in Harris' plans. Again, this chapter had my kids and I rolling with laughter. Probably because 6th graders think groin injuries are the funniest thing. The boys use the two horses for different capers. One was used for a landing spot after they swung out of the barn loft, and the other for a "Gene Autry" moment. After the second caper soured, "Me" was talked into taking the blame for the incident. That planted the seed of revenge.

Chapter 9:   It was nice to have this chapter in the book. It showed us that this family really does have loving feelings for each other. Harris accidentally got hit by a bull and was nearly killed. Knute came to his rescue and ended up breaking his arm. Claire took over and gave them both the attention they needed. Harris milked his injury for all that it was worth, which made "Me" have to work that much harder on the farm and that much more bent on revenge.

Chapter 10:   "Me" falls in love only to have Harris ruin it. It figures, doesn't it? There were chapters in this book that were so funny that I didn't think anything could beat them. Until I read this one. My class made me read the section of this chapter that had to do with another groin injury. But I have to admit, I can't remember anything so funny. The conversation between the two boys before the action is hilarious! Gary Paulsen definitely has a way with words. "Me" is finally able to get his revenge by having Harris pee on an electrical wire. The reward being that Harris would get to have two dirty pictures that "Me" had brought with him to the Larson's. During the first second, everything is fine. However during the next second, lightening hit. (So to speak!)

Chapter 11:   Instead of taking a nice, leisurely bike ride, the boys decide to rig up the washing machine motor to the bike. Instant motorcycle! What else could possibly go wrong? Well, this project actually went pretty much according to plan. In a way, Harris reminds me of me! Sometimes I just can't leave well-enough alone. I have to have bigger, better, faster, etc. Some people would call this the "Tim, the tool-man, Taylor" syndrome. He is the main character on the show "Home Improvement," and is never satisfied with mediocrity.

Chapter 12:   The final chapter really pulls at your heart strings. Finally "Me" has found a home in which he is happy. A good home. He feels bonds with this family, as the family does with him. Louie has even carved a figure of "Me" and added it to his village. He also feels love for these people. Those feelings are reciprocated also. The fact that "Me" has to leave is heartbreaking. I'm sure my kids didn't think that the story would end this way. Don't all books end with a happy ending? It's good to expose them to some books that don't end with, ". . . and they lived happily every after."

Questions for Discussion

1) Would you have wanted to leave the Larson's farm after the first day? Explain.

2) Describe Harris' relationship with each member of his family.

3) How do you feel about Harris smoking? Why?

4) Do you know someone who has done crazy things like Harris? What did they do?

5) Would you have kept following along with Harris' schemes? Why?

6) Which of Harris and "Me" 's antics do you think were safe? Were hazardous? In what ways could they have changed the more dangerous stunts into safe ones, but still fun?

7) "Me" seemed to fit into the Larson's family. Do you think you would have? Explain.

8) Why do you think Harris pulled so many crazy stunts?

9) Did Harris like having "Me" around? Did they become as close as brothers?

10) How are the women's roles in the book diffrent from women's roles today?

11) What kind of feelings would you have had while leaving the Larson's with the Deputy? Try to explain them.

12) If you had to place Harris in a home, where and with whom would it be? Why?

13) Do you think the author lived a similar life to Harris? To "Me"? Explain.

14) How do you think the author came up with the ideas for this book?

15) How would you have ended the book?

Activities

1) Write a letter to the Sheriff's Department in the book, explaining where you think "Me" should live.

2) Write another chapter to the book with another crazy plan that the boys try.

3) Write a response to Harris' letter at the end of the book.

4) Rewrite the ending of the book, the way you would like to see it end.

5) Study the math and physics of the boys' capers. See if their stunts would have been possible in real life and include any changes that you would make.

6) Put together a mini-skit to promote the reading of this book.

7) Have a speaker come in to talk to the students about foster homes,

orphanages, adoption, and where/how children are placed when there are problems in the home.

8) Begin writing letters to children who might be in "Me"'s position.

9) Contact an organization such as Big Brothers, Big Sisters, to see if a field trip or special activity could be planned with children of their organization.

10) Do an author study of Gary Paulsen.

About the Author: Gary Paulsen is one of America's most popular writers for young people, and his books have won numerous awards, including three Newbery Honors. He has made his Harcourt Brace debut with two adult titles: *Clabbered Dirt, Sweet Grass* (1992) and the first book of his memoirs, *Eastern Sun, Winter Moon* (1993). He lives with his wife, painter Ruth Wright Paulsen, on their ranch in New Mexico. ∎

∎ This nontraditional undergraduate student wrote a reading autobiography, in which she reflected upon her own reading. She also wrote a response to a professional book, *Readers' Workshop* by Pat Hagerty.

This student has children of her own and has spent a lot of time in classrooms. She has a sense of children's reading because she listens to and observes children, both in her role as a parent and in that of a classroom aide. Because of this, her notions about reading may differ from those of a more traditional student who has not spent much time with children in a home or school environment. Her insights into her own reading, as well as the reading of children, show who she is as a reader and who she will be as a teacher of reading.

I begin this section with my reading autobiography because I feel that exploring my own reading process helped reveal to me how I want to teach reading and language arts. I went to grade school during a very traditional time, but it did not put a damper on my love of literature because I was offered so many wonderful books in my home and encouraged to explore the libraries in school and town. This has become the key to my philosophy of teaching reading and language arts. I will immerse my students in good literature and have it always at their fingertips.

Reading Readers' Workshop *by Pat Hagerty changed my paradigm about reading and language arts. I have a wealth of new ideas that I am excited to try because they are based upon what really works for children. Thanks for requiring us to read "real books" and not just boring textbooks.*

Reading Autobiography

I prefaced this autobiography with copies from my childhood nursery rhymes book, because they symbolize my earliest memories of reading. I used to gaze endlessly through the door that the mother is holding open for her child. I still feel the same wonder when I approach a new book. The experience remains magical and mysterious. The rhymes that my mother read to me over and over again were an important part of my learning to read later at six years old.

I still remember some of the small picture books that my mother read to me. It was an important part of my life, especially on Saturday nights when reading was accompanied by popcorn and 7-Up. I know that these picture books established a love for literature and a burning desire to read!

I thought I would perish before I reached first grade when I would finally be allowed to read. When it finally came, I learned fast and my friend Kathy Owens and I would sit in the back of the room during other reading group sessions, and race through our Dick and Jane books. I'm amazed it didn't bore me to death to have nothing but Dick and Jane, but I'm convinced that the richness of literature in my home kept me interested.

I recall being sent to the small library in my grade school on the pretense that I was to dust the books. I'm sure my teachers knew I would end up sitting and reading instead, but they knew that was better than having me sit idly at my desk, waiting for the other students to finish their work. This is a fond memory and I can still see the rows of books which always held the allure of buried treasure. I felt the same way about the town library where I would go sometimes to wait for my mother to pick me up. These libraries and caring teachers helped promote my literacy to a large degree.

My love of books grew with the passage of time. I remember devouring every Nancy Drew Mystery that I could get my hands and eyes on. I recall favorites like The Yearling and The Secret Garden.

My fascination with literature led me to the University of Nebraska where I obtained a B.A. in English Literature. This is where the sad part comes in, and I never understood what happened until I returned to school the second time. I literally burned out on analyzing literature. I still remember being in trouble with one of my professors for suggesting that we were analyzing a beautiful poem to death. My new experience is that we can now allow for an aesthetic response to literature instead of a purely critical, analytical response.

My love for reading hasn't faded and I've continued to choose books from good literature reviews and from recommendations.

I feel that understanding my lifelong reading journey will help me give my students a love of reading that will last their lifetimes.

Response to *Readers' Workshop*

The most important part of this book for me is Pat Hagerty's basic premise that children should have free choice of the literature they are reading. My personal experience with my own children and with the elementary children I worked with last year, is that children are the most excited about the books they choose themselves. I really like the child-centered approach that is presented in this book. But I have also wondered how or even if I will be able to put these techniques into practice if I am required to use a basal reader. Some of the workshop elements, particularly responding, could still be incorporated. Mini-lessons and share sessions could also be used. I know that I would like to create time each day for the workshop approach and could use library books throughout the week.

This book is so clearly written and contains such a wealth of ideas. I especially liked the specific guidelines about asking questions. I feel that questions can either promote or close down a child's learning process and are a very important consideration.

I was impressed by Ms. Hagerty's insistence that sharing is essential. I know that I have been writing more because of the sharing done in our classroom. I also have been sharing withmy family which has stimulated them to write and share. This process is exciting for me so I know that most kids would be excited about it also.

Finally, I liked her cooperative approach to assessment. I think that children benefit from being part of the assessment process. They also benefit from setting their own goals so that they become independent thinkers and readers.

I am happy to have this and the other books Ms. Hagerty has referenced as a resource. Even if I'm tied to a basal reader I intend to involve the children in these kinds of activities so that reading belongs to them rather than to me. ∎

∎ This first-year teacher is a reader. She was distraught to find that her new classroom did not have any books in it. Although she had collected many picture books, she decided she needed more chapter books for her fourth-grade students. And she decided that she needed to read more novels for children so that she could recommend good books to her students. She wrote her own reading goals, which include her desire to read more chapter books, as well as to stay informed professionally in the area of language arts. She recognizes the importance of reading for pleasure and reading for information, and models these types of reading for her students. The notion of setting reading goals is another process she models for her own students, who can then set their own reading goals.

Reading has always been important to me. I have fond memories of going to the bookstore, library, and ordering from book clubs when I was young. Simply put, I love to read! I read everyday for pleasure. There is always at least one book next to my bed. No matter how tired I am, I have to read at least a page of something before I go to bed. Sometimes this gets me in trouble and I read for too long.

Everyday at school we read silently for fifteen minutes. On Wednesday, we read for thirty minutes. Sometimes I think I look forward to RESBY (Read Excellent Stories By Yourself) time more than the students do. We have a large reading center in the classroom with a couch and many pillows. I want my students to be comfortable while they read. A sign should have been posted in the classroom the first time I walked in: Books Not Included. When I found out I would be teaching fourth grade, I frantically started buying books other than picture books. I finally went to a used bookstore and bought many chapter books for the room. The kids decided how we were going to arrange them in the reading carousel and shelves. They came up with a much better system than I did, of course. What is so amazing is that many of my students have been bringing in their own books to add to the reading center. This tells me that they are beginning to see reading as fun and are in the process of becoming lifelong readers.

I have included my reading goals in this section. I feel that I need to read more books that my students would find appealing. I need to serve as a better resource for them to help them find good books. I also need to read more professional literature so that I continue to grow and improve as a teacher. These goals will be modeled for my students as I ask them to set their own personal reading goals this year.

Reading Goals

I have never set an attainable, short-term goal for myself. I have told myself in the past that I would do X by a certain date, but I rarely would reach it. I believe the most important reason why I never reached past goals was the lack of desire to do the work involved. If you do not have a strong desire to do something, you are not going to do it. This is true for everyone.

The following are two reading goals that I have set for myself for the next year.

Goal: To Become More Familiar with Books for Intermediate Grade Students

I have spent most of my time reading and learning about picture books. They are my weakness! I must have considerable self-control when I am in a bookstore. Since I am currently teaching fourth grade, and think that I will next year, I want to have a larger knowledge base of chapter books. I strongly believe picture books are appropriate for any grade. We use picture books all the time in our classroom. However, my students enjoy children's books because they are able to read and enjoy them. I feel bad because I do not know that many books to recommend to them.

I plan on reaching this goal by continuing to read chapter books during our daily RESBY (Read Excellent Stories By Yourself) time, before I go to bed (my favorite reading time), order books out of book orders, and to browse more often in the chapter book section of libraries and bookstores.

Goal: Read More Journal Articles, Especially Those in the Area of Language Arts

I believe it is important to be knowledgeable of current research in your profession. It is an essential element of a professional. This is an area I believe educators are at fault. Many do not read good journal articles and are therefore, unaware of new teaching methods and ideas. In other professions such as the medical, law, and computer fields, keeping current by reading journals and magazines is essential in order to be an effective professional.

I plan to reach this goal by reading *The Reading Teacher* that I receive and other articles that I come across or other teachers mention. ▮

▮ This reflection and its artifacts are the work of a student in secondary English/language arts methods, an undergraduate course taken, in this case, by a nontraditional student returning to college after a successful business career because she had a passion to teach speech. These particular artifacts addressed the theme "I am a reader," and reflect this student's strong sense of herself as a reader.

I included this artifact because it illustrates throughout who I am as a reader. I am a reader who constantly seeks to make sense of what I encounter, whether that is in terms of text, or discussion. I am a lifelong reader.

September 21, 1995

"Lifetime readers are made, not born." This seems like such a simple thought, but the whole concept of creating a lifetime reader consumed a large portion of the discussion today. Dr. Rogers had us separate into two groups and we were each provided with the same article about developing lifetime readers, and also a "reading rubric" against which we viewed the article. We almost immediately got hung up on the idea of the teacher developing "ways of making reading more attractive to our students . . ." Here we were somewhat split, with several members of the group speaking on a personal level about how much they dislike reading, and how the outcomes listed in the rubric would have no effect on those students who enter your classroom with a pre-disposition to dislike reading assignments. Over the years I have come to re-alize that there are numerous people who have read many more books than I have, and for a long time I worried that somehow the numbers made me "less" of a reader. But I know that my desire to read is still as strong today, as it was when I was in grade school, and that no one can take away from me. I am a lifetime reader, and I want to find a way to encourage that in each of my students.

October 12, 1995

"What is an educated person? It is someone who knows what to do when they don't know what to do." This was actually a quote that was thrown out last week during our discussion about our upcoming practicums. It didn't really sink in until today. Dr. Rogers was talking about the types of activities that she would like to see us use in our practicums. She used terms like "writing invita-tions," "discussion invitations," and "writing and speaking activity," and I panicked. I didn't have a clue what she was talking about, and since none of my fellow classmates were asking questions, I assumed I was the only one in the room that didn't understand. So I asked what she meant. Was I miss-

ing something? Were these "things" that you learned if you were going to be an English teacher, and therefore I had missed out? But as she spoke in answer to my concerns, it suddenly dawned on me that I knew what to do. I simply had not connected what I knew, to the expressions she had used. "What is an educated person?" I think that the more appropriate response would be, "It is someone who *can figure out* what to do when they don't know what to do."

> READING a book is like re-writing it for yourself . . . You bring to a
> novel, anything you read, all your experiences of the world. You
> bring your history and you read it in your own terms.
> *Angela Carter* (1940–92), *British Author*

Reading Is:

September 13, 1994: According to my Webster's College Dictionary, reading is "1) the action or practice of a person who reads; 2) the oral interpretation of written language; 3) the interpretation given in the performance of a dramatic part, musical composition, etc; 4) the extent to which a person had read; literally knowledge; and so forth."

Reading Is:

September 21, 1994: Reading is about sharing something that you have read with someone else. *The Precious Present* by Spencer Johnson, M.D., is that kind of a book for me. The first time that I read this book was in March, 1989. It was a gift from my boss and dear friend, J. J. I've read the book many, many times since. It normally sits on my nightstand where I can read it whenever I begin to lose sight of what's important. Its words keep me grounded.

I've read the book with each of my children. My son had just turned 14 the first time we read it together. I say the first time, because we've read it together many times since. The last time was just before I moved back to Nebraska in December 1993. My son decided to stay in New Jersey to attend school and be near his girlfriend. Reading the book together one last time was a good reminder for both of us to focus on the present and not look back.

I've bought additional copies of the book that I plan to give to my children when the time is right. I hope someday that they will share the book with their children, or someone that they love.

Reading Is:

September 29, 1994: Reading is about living in a learning environment. It is about being willing to "teach" yourself. It is about always learning new concepts and ideas. When I was given the opportunity to assist the Communication Department with the UNO Speech Tournament, I suddenly realized how little I knew about the formal speech competition. So I spent quite a bit of time in the library and I found a wide range of sources.

Reading Is:

October 2, 1994: Reading is about wanting more of what you have seen or heard. Today at the UNO Speech Tournament, I heard several outstanding oral interpretations of prose and poetry by a variety of authors. I plan to find and read more by author Miguel Pinero. I understand that he had two books, *Nuyorican Poetry*, and *Short Eyese*.

Reading Is:

October 4, 1994: Reading is about creating new paradigms, shifting old ones, or confirming existing ones. As a teacher, I want to encourage my students to look at all sides of an issue. For my Argumentation and Debate class, I was required to develop an argument for a Town Hall Meeting on Capital Punishment. Although I did not support the position that I was required to argue, I found that by reading as much as I could on both sides of the issue, I was able to fairly represent that position I was assigned.

Reading Is:

October 5, 1994: Reading is about learning from a variety of sources. As both a Business and Speech teacher, I want my students to be able to use a wide range of sources to learn about issues. For Human Relations, we were required to read and evaluate five articles from journals and magazines that are written by and/or for different ethnic groups. My supplemental reading evaluations came from magazines like E*bony* and from scholarly journals like *American Indian and Alaska Native Mental Health Research*. I want to be able to instill in my students a desire to read about issues that they might not otherwise spend much time thinking about, and to use sources that they might not otherwise use.

Reading Is:

October 13, 1994: Reading is about growing as a person and a professional.

Reading Is:

October 21, 1994: Reading is about technology. With access to the Internet, we have expanded the number of books, magazines, and newspapers that we can read. For Instructional Systems, I researched a topic using only Internet resources. I believe that using technology doesn't decrease the opportunities to read, but rather increases those opportunties.

Reading Is:

October 21, 1994: Reading is about being passionate.

Reading Is:

October 27, 1994: Reading is a class I take at UNO where I am learning how to incorporate reading and writing into my content-area classes. Reading is about learning new and different ways to help your students. Reading is about literacy.

Reading Is:

November 9, 1994: Reading is about preparing to teach a lesson that will engage all of the students. Reading is researching a subject or concept. Reading is looking at alternative sources of information.

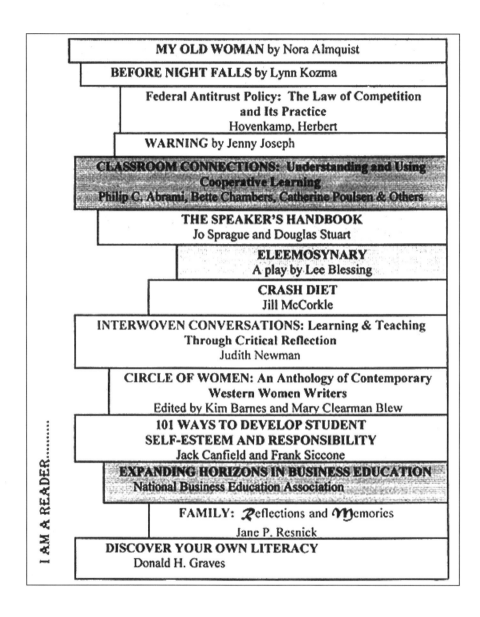

MY OLD WOMAN by Nora Almquist

BEFORE NIGHT FALLS by Lynn Kozma

Federal Antitrust Policy: The Law of Competition and Its Practice
Hovenkamp, Herbert

WARNING by Jenny Joseph

CLASSROOM CONNECTIONS: Understanding and Using Cooperative Learning
Philip C. Abrami, Bette Chambers, Catherine Poulsen & Others

THE SPEAKER'S HANDBOOK
Jo Sprague and Douglas Stuart

ELEEMOSYNARY
A play by Lee Blessing

CRASH DIET
Jill McCorkle

INTERWOVEN CONVERSATIONS: Learning & Teaching Through Critical Reflection
Judith Newman

CIRCLE OF WOMEN: An Anthology of Contemporary Western Women Writers
Edited by Kim Barnes and Mary Clearman Blew

101 WAYS TO DEVELOP STUDENT SELF-ESTEEM AND RESPONSIBILITY
Jack Canfield and Frank Siccone

EXPANDING HORIZONS IN BUSINESS EDUCATION
National Business Education Association

FAMILY: Reflections and Memories
Jane P. Resnick

DISCOVER YOUR OWN LITERACY
Donald H. Graves

I AM A READER.........

▌ The artifact and reflection that follow were from a portfolio in Sheri's Adolescent Literature course. Students were asked to represent the twenty titles they chose to read during the semester in some manner that would help them remember the specific titles. Any form of artifact was acceptable.

This graduate student represented each of the twenty titles she read by writing about the metaphors in a particular work in order to capture and remember the titles.

I am a reader who engages with what I read. I am not content to merely read The Chocolate War—*I have to see what I can discern from the reading that will help me with future content. I want to be able to keep track of my reading in such a way that I can use the information I garner later, with my students. I also read a lot so I need to find a way to remember what I've read. I do this by writing extensively about my reading. This artifact shows this about me.*

The Chocolate War by Robert Cormier

I never doubted for a second that Archie would get what was coming to him. The villain never wins in the end, right? Wrong. I get the feeling that most people probably connect with Jerry Renault, and cheer him on through the whole book. I certainly did. The poster that hung in his locker—"do I dare disturb the universe?"—seemed to foreshadow his actions in that he went against the Trinity system. Simply because of that poster I expected Jerry to come out on top of Archie in the end. I mean, what was the point of the marbles if Archie always chose the white ones? Every part of the book that led me in one direction was just a tease. That was the one reason that I like this book so much and why I finished it in less than a day. Cormier surprised me around every corner. Nothing was like it appeared, and the good guy never won.

Even when the book was finished, Cormier left many things unresolved. For instance—what happened to Jerry? Was he hurt badly? Did Obie ever get revenge on Archie? Why did Brother Leon need the money from the chocolate sale? Did things at Trinity change after the chocolate war? Did the Vigils still control the school after Archie was publicly challenged?

The fact that Cormier left all the questions unanswered makes sense. It kept me thinking about the book for days afterward. I even dreamed about Jerry lying in the hospital the night I got done reading the book. Because Cormier hadn't given me the answers I wanted, I had to resolve the book myself. This way everyone gets their own custom-made ending.

One of the things that really struck me about Cormier's *The Chocolate War* was his use of metaphors. Cormier is a very descriptive author, and many of his most powerful images come from the use of metaphors. Most likely he uses this tactic to compress space in the book, because if he used realistic detail, the text would be much longer. Whatever his reasoning, it is effective and lends a lot to the passages in the book—it especially lends insight into the characters. We are able to identify with the characers in a way a reader usually can't because Cormier ties them directly with things we are familiar with.

Some of my favorite metaphoric phrases from the book:

> As he turned to take the ball, a dam burst against the side of his head and a hand grenade shattered his stomach. Engulfed by nausea, he pitched toward the grass. His mouth encountered gravel, and he spat frantically, afraid that some of his teeth had been knocked out. Rising to his feet, he saw the field through drifting gauze but held on until everything settled into place, like a lens focusing, making the world sharp again, with edges. (description of football practice)

> The wind rose, kicking puffs of dust from the football field. The field needed seeding. The bleachers also needed attention— they sagged, peeling paint like leprosy on the benches. The shadows of the goal posts sprawled on the field like grotesque crosses.

> He's earned his job as Assigner because of his quick mind, his swift intelligence, his fertile imagination, his ability to see two moves ahead as if life were a giant checker or chess game. (description of Archie)

> Often he rose early in the morning, before anyone else, and poured himself liquid through sunrise streets, and everything seemed beautiful everything in it's proper orbit, nothing impossible, the entire world attainable. (description of Goober)

> Jerry's hands were joined like a duck's bill waiting to swallow the ball. . .He saw Carter snaking through the line again, like some monstrous reptile in his helmet, but suddenly Carter became all

arms and legs tossing and turning in the air. . .both of them fell into a tangle of bodies. (football practice)

Etc., Etc., Etc., Cormier's metaphors go on and on, I have hardly enough typing paper to write them all. But these amply demonstrate his effectiveness. ▌

▌ This artifact and reflection are from the portfolio of a student in Adolescent Literature. This graduate student is a teacher who wanted to keep track of specific titles, genres, and themes. Organization, one of the key characteristics of this student, was vital to her entire portfolio, as this artifact illustrates.

I included this particular artifact in the "Who I Am as Reader" section because it shows not only what I read, but how I organize my reading list. I like to know the topics "covered" by a book for later reference, and I like to know if I can use it in my teaching, hence the last column. I've read 92 books this semester, not bad, huh? I guess I see what is possible when you get to read what you want and have a genuine interest in. Thanks.

TITLE	AUTHOR	TOPICS	FOR 1-8 LMC?
Abbi, My Love		suicide	
Across Five Aprils	Hunt	Civil War	yes
After the Rain	Mazer	death	jr. high
Am I Blue	various	homosexual themes	no
Annie's Promise	Levitin	historical fiction	yes
Baseball in April	Soto	sports	yes
Bill	Reaver	dog story	yes
Bodies in the Besseldorf Motel	Naylor		
Brave	Lipsyte	boxing, male theme	jr. high
But I'll Be Back Again	Rylant	autobiography	

But I'll Be Back Again	Rylant	autobiography	
Charlotte Sometimes		fantasy	yes
Cheater Cheater	Levy	school cheating, friendship	yes
Christmas Sonata	Paulsen		yes
Close Enough to Touch	Peck		no
Contender	Lipsyte	male theme	jr. high
Crossing	Paulsen		no
Dark Stairs	Byars		
Daughters of Eve	Duncan		no
Dear Mom, Get Me Out of Here	Conford		jr. high
Devils's Bridge	DeFelice	mystery, fishing	yes
Diamond in the Window	Langton		
Dicey's Song	Voigt		jr. high
Downriver	Hobbs		jr. high
Dragon Wings	Yep		yes
Duplicate	Sleater		
Durango Street		gangs	
Enter Three Witches	Gilmore		no
Finding Buck McHenry	Slote	baseball, Am. Negro League	yes
Fine White Dust	Rylant		
Fling	Thomas		
Flip-flop Girl	Paterson		yes
For the Love of Pete	Morino	Aging, missing fathers	no
Fredrich		Jewish religion, WWII	
Ghosts Don't Get Goosebumps	Woodruff		
Girl in the Box		mystery	no
Hannah In Between	Rodowski		jr. high
Heartlight	Baron		
Homecoming	Voigt		jr. high
House of Dies Drier	Hamilton	underground railroad	jr. high
Hundred Dresses	Estes		yes

In My Father's House		historical fiction, Civil War	
Into the Dream	Sleater	science fiction	
Jim Dandy	Irwin	historical fiction	yes
Journey to America	Levitin	historical fiction	yes
Juniper Game			?
Kindness	Rylant		
Letters from the Inside	Marsden		no
Letters to Rifka		diary	yes
Mandy	Edwards	(Julie Andrews)	yes
Monster's Ring	Coville	mystery	yes
Night of the Twisters	Ruckman	tornado, adventure	yes
NightJohn	Paulsen	slavery	jr. high
No Time to Cry	McDaniel		jr. high
Not On a White Horse			no
Ode to the Neighborhood	Soto		
One Fat Summer	Lipsyte		jr. high
Other Side of Dark	Nixon	movie "Awake to Danger"	no
Owl in Love			
Popcorn Days and Buttermilk Nights	Paulsen		yes
Revolutions of the Heart			
Runner	Voigt		jr. high
Screaming High		drug trafficking	read-aloud
Show Me the Evidence	Ferguson		no
Silver Days	Levitin	historical fiction	yes
So Long at the Fair	Irwin	suicide	
Solitary Blue	Voigt		
Somewhere in Darkness	Meyers		no
Songs in the Silence	Murphy	whales, family	yes
Sparrow Hawk Red	Michaelson		yes
Star Fisher		historical fiction, Chinese	yes
Staying Fat for Sarah Byrns	Crutcher		

Strange New Feelings	Lester	slavery	
Strange Night Writings of Jessimine Colter	DeFelice	science fiction	yes
Sudden Silence	Bunting		jr. high
Tent	Paulsen		
Those Summer Girls I Never Met			no
Thunder Rolling in the Mountains	O'Dell	historical fiction, Native Americans	yes
Travel Far, Pay No Fare	Lindbergh	fantasy	yes
Trouble With Lemons	Hayes, D.		
Tunes For Bears To Dance To	Cormier		?
Twins	Cooney	mystery	
Twisted Window	Duncan	mystery	jr. high
Two Weeks with the Queen	Glitzman	death	jr. high
Waiting for the Rain		South Africa	
Weekend Was Murder	Nixon	murder mystery	
Westing Game		thinking skills	yes
Wild Children			jr. high
Wind Blows Backwards	Hahn		no
Year of Impossible Good-byes			
Year Without Michael			
Zlata's Diary		Bosnia War	yes

▌ This reflection and artifact are from the portfolio of an undergraduate student in Sheri's Adolescent Literature course. This particular section was from the "I Am a Reader" portion of the portfolio, illustrating the connection possibilities the literature we read in the course had beyond the course.

I included this artifact because it illustrates who I am as a reader. I read Chris Crutcher's book and it reminded me of a poem, which I had to hunt for some time to find. I am a reader who makes connections between what they read and what they have read before.

> After I read Chris Crutcher's book *Chinese Handcuffs*, I was reminded of a poem that I have loved since—well, I don't know since when, but it's been a long, long time . . .

Attics of My Life

In the attics of my life
Full of cloudy dreams unreal
Full of tastes no tongue can know
And lights no eye can see
    When there was no ear to hear
    You sang to me

I have spent my life
Seeking all that's still unsung
Bent my ear to hear the tune
And closed my eye to see
    When there were no strings to play
    You played to me

In the book of love's own dream
Where all the print is blood
Where all the pages are my days
And all my lights grow old
    When I had no wings to fly
    You flew to me

In the secret space of dreams
Where I dreaming lay amazed
When the secrets all are told
And the petals all unfold
    When there was no dream of mine
    You dreamed of me ▌

▌ The student who wrote the following reflection and artifacts was in two of Sheri's courses concurrently: English/Language Arts Methods and Teaching English Linguistically. This particular set of artifacts came from the "I Am a Reader" section. The student was a traditional twenty-two-year-old senior, just shy of student teaching. She was quite a reader coming into the course, and left with a renewed interest in writing and portfolios. Introducing portfolios into her student teaching experience the next semester, she used not only what she had read to reflect in written format, but also practiced what she read, wrote, and believed.

I included this set of artifacts to represent who I am as a reader. I am a reader who selects meaningful and useful readings, and then writes about them in order to make further sense of the readings. Two important elements in my teaching philosophy are evident in this artifact: 1) I believe choice is very important in determining what is important enough to read, and 2) I think one needs to write to make sense of what one thinks about something one has read. Both of these are part of who I am as a reader. I will want the same for my students.

For my professional readings, I wanted to read about actual situations and problems with English curriculum in the classroom. While reading numerous selections in *English Journal*, I realized I was drawing connections between my classes I am enrolled in as well as questions I found myself asking about my future teaching experiences. I was very interested in reading about how various activities such as portfolios or group work involved the students or were advantages to them.

I will summarize my readings as well as bring up thoughts or reactions to what I read. It felt really good to be able to draw connections to what we have learned in Methods and Teaching English Linguistically and what is actually being implemented in today's classrooms.

Selection taken from:

English Journal, Feb. 1990, Vol. 79, No. 2
English Journal, Sept. 1992, Vol. 81, No. 5

"Literature and Teaching: Getting Our Knowledge into Our Bones" by Bill Martin

Bill Martin does an excellent job describing what he feels is "knowing something in my bones." This becomes a phrase he associated with the teaching of literature. Martin outlines various objectives to consider when teaching literature or writing about literature. It is important for students to *experience* the literature, not just recite quotes or irrelevant characters.

Martin's teaching style and his values impressed me a great deal. He favored an atmosphere in which *both* the teacher and student are in a learning environment. Rigorous grading and seriousness had no place in the classroom (seriousness meaning no relaxed discussions or informal settings).

As I was reading this article, I began to think of how I wanted to construct my student teaching classroom. Feedback from the teacher as well as from the students is of utmost importance to me. I want to be a model of learning, not just a teacher-figure. One of Martin's goals for his classroom states "we should support each other in reading rather than compete with each other." I intend for my students to give me their interests, ideas and thoughts on what they have read. I, too, will work on giving my opinions (although not to distract students from the material) on what is being read. This sharing will show students firsthand that I am not in the classroom to control them or teach them monotonous material. Learning will be mutual among the students and the teacher.

In summary, Martin explains that we as teachers also need to listen for ideas from students. He emphasized a continual learning environment to make it possible for the student "to discuss the journey they have taken with the text."

This article may as well have been taken from *Discover Your Own Literacy* by Donald Graves. I drew many connections between the ongoing learning and listening environment in both Martin's article and Graves' book. I am glad these authors discuss such an environment in their writings. I am beginning to build my teaching values on these techiques.

"Literature Discussion: A Classroom Environment for Thinking and Sharing" by Elizabeth Egan Close

Elizabeth Close, a Language Arts instructor at Farnsworth Middle School in New York and researcher, shared outstanding strategies to implement literature discussion in the classroom. According to Close, literary discussion does not necessarily have to begin with discussion of a book. Close explains "Establishing that environment of trust has become one of (my) first concerns at the beginning of the year."

As we have demonstrated in our Methods and Teaching English Linguistically classes, it takes a lot of trust among peers to read writings of both a scholastic and personal nature. We took part in various activities which helped us get to know each other and build a learning community. Close suggests teachers should implement activities such as interviewing and sharing unique qualilties about each other.

Asking questions was a part of the lesson which was important to Close. Students would get into groups and compile a list of questions they felt deserved discussion. This activity shows the class that every question is important and each inquiry will be discussed among students. By forming questions in groups, students may not feel as intimidated to ask questions by themselves. I could see how easily discussion can be prompted when working in groups. Formulating and presenting questions to the class will become routine.

I feel building trust and a learning community is the basis for healthy discussions. When students feel comfortable with their learning environment, they will be much more likely to share their ideas or concerns with the rest of the class.

"The Fragile Inclination to Write: Praise and Criticism in the Classroom" by Linda Miller Cleary

Linda Cleary outlines excellent ideas on grading, praising and giving feedback on papers. She holds tight to her belief that it is important to *encourage* writing with students. Students' motivation and outlook on writing can change as a result of just one bad comment or critical remark.

As I was reading this article, I felt the importance of a student's paper should be the ideas they have incorporated in their paper and what they have learned. Cleary used several students' responses in her article about how they felt when they received a grade or negative comment on a paper. One student commented, "I don't get excited about (writing). I do it because I know it had to be done. I think I know what my teachers want from me now." Methods class discussed this exact problem. Students tend to write what they feel the instructor wants to hear. When teachers give their students that impression, students lose out on the chance to express themselves and write their true feelings.

One girl in this article made me think of a particular student in Methods and Linguistics. The girl in the article stated, "I wrote a biography of my grandfather. I worked so hard. I learned so much. She (the teacher) had all these criticisms that were primarily mechanical things, like long paragraphs and five-line sentences. Now I try to do what she wants and I resent it." This made me think how this teacher had hurt this student's pride and self-esteem. This biography had to be personal and the teacher was basically telling her it was wrong.

Finally, Close wrote about students writing for curiosity. Her students described how they interviewed people about questions they had in society or about laws or career choices. Cleary felt the students learned about themselves because they had to dig deep for the information. Not only did they learn more from this activity, but the students were interested more in what they were doing, so their hearts were in their writing. The interest level makes all the difference in the world.

"Adapting the Portfolio to Meet the Students Needs" by Margie Krest

Portfolios, in Margie Krest's class, are used much like we use them in Methods class. Krest's class uses them solely for the writing students have completed throughout the course of the semester. Her portfolios can be used to gauge that progress of students' compositions. Her students take the portfolio assignment very seriously. Because they know they are being graded on progress and learning, a great deal of effort is put into each piece of writing for the portfolio.

Krest has seen very beneficial results from assigning a portfolio for the semester. First, students are proud of the work they have completed because they know it is a reflection of them. Secondly, students enjoy seeing their portfolios grow throughout the semester. Rather than throwing papers away after they have been graded, students are now filing them in the portfolio and literally watching their progress in the classroom. Finally, parents and administrators can see the writing students have done and the effort they put into their writing.

Krest does teach three different levels of English, and, therefore, must adapt her grading scale to the advanced as well as the lower-level students. In order to meet the needs of the various levels of students, Krest gives two grades: one for the portfolio collection itself and one grade for the revisions and drafts of the papers. If the students need more help in writing, she will raise the weight of the drafts and revision sections so those students can work harder at improving their work.

Part of the portfolio grading system is revisions. Students are asked to not just correct grammatical errors, but change the mode of paper (e.g., change a descriptive paper to a persuasive paper). This may be challenging for the student, but they are able to develop writing skills in an area they may not be too familiar with.

From this piece, I have learned how students can become excited about their writing and can keep the spark of interest going when writing a paper. Portfolios are proof of learning, and when a student knows they have improved, that is when they feel confident in themselves.

"Sharing Standard English: Whose Standard?" by Linda Christensen

This article became of great interest to me since Standard English is a topic we've discussed in class throughout the semester. Christensen explained her experiences with Standard English. She had been laughed at, corrected and told many times that her English was "wrong." Christensen remarks that "Students need to know where to find help. . .and they need to learn that in a context that doesn't say 'the way you said this is wrong.'" I liked how Christensen explained that the context of the message is what is important, not just how it is said. Many people find other words to replace what they want to say for lack of "correct" pronunciation. When students take this approach to speaking, they lose their own expression.

Christensen did not write about what is or is not Standard English, but rather how to deal with students who refuse to write because they are embarrassed of the way they speak. In order to get students to "reach out" with their writing, a certain level of trust needs to be established in the classroom. To obtain this level of trust, Christensen brings in former students of hers to read personal writings. From this sharing, students learn that expressing their thoughts on paper is the most important focus, not how it is written. Students can draw connections from their own lives to the lives of their peers. I feel that I can share my writings with others in my class because we have so many people sharing their feelings and compositions. This really does create a writing community because trust is established as well as a comfort level where students feel at ease reading in front of the class. ▮

▮ Reading autobiographies is a requirement in Sheri's English/Language Arts Methods course. While the writing is required, it is also some of the most meaningful writing my students and I do; I know because they've told me so. Nowhere is that more true than in this artifact and reflection. The individual writer had a clinically schizophrenic mother who appeared often in this student's writing. Additionally, she thought often of this background as she watched her own students, and as she student-taught at the same time she took this methods course. The struggles her students had were reflected in this artifact, in which the power to empathize is forcefully felt and expressed.

I've included my reading autobiography to illustrate who I am as a reader. I am a reader who has learned from her mistreatment as a child and will never label my future students as a result. As I say in my closing line, I want to concentrate on helping prisoners of illiteracy achieve parole. This desire fuels who I am as a reader.

Literacy

Reading, a Painful Process
8/29/94

The students in my seventh-period class have trouble with reading; they're freshmen who find reading fourth-grade material painfully difficult. As I sat watching them, a torrent of memories ruptured an imaginary dam created long ago, and forgotten hurt washed over me, almost forcing an audible gasp for breath like that of a drowning swimmer. I didn't read until I was in the fourth grade and, like them, was intimately acquainted with shame, humiliation, and frustration, the constant companions of the less than literate.

Elementary school was hell for me. Mrs. B., Mrs. H., and Mrs. M., grande dames of B. B. Elementary, conferred and the sentence was unanimous—I was retarded, no doubt about it. I knew they thought me stupid and I agreed. I was saved from a life term as an illiterate by my grandparents, who raised me, and refused to believe them. Grandpa took me to a university where an IQ test was performed. The experts concluded that I was actually sort of bright, noting that important academic windows had been missed because mom's schizophrenia kept our house in a general uproar. This data was forwarded to the school.

My oddessy began with placement in Mrs. C.'s remedial reading class. She was beautiful, tall, and slim with glorious flaming hair always worn up and wonderful amber eyes. I adored the woman; she was my hero and, miraculously, less than a month after placement, I learned to read. Mrs. B., Mrs. H., and Mrs. M. refused to believe that an intellectual journey was in progress, but it was. It began with phonics, moved to Disney stories, progressed to Black and Flame, meandered through Nancy Drew and Cherry someone who was a nurse and continued. I read dictionaries, encyclopedias, aspirin boxes . . . anything with print.

Other elementary students still thought I was weird, and in all truth, I was. I was an only child and mom screaming around the house wasn't conducive to forming lasting friendships. I hated being unpopular; it made me miserable, but once I learned to read, they could no longer call me weird and dumb. Mrs. C. saved my life by opening a world I could escape to by cracking the cover of a book.

Things were better in junior high—I had two best friends, who weren't weird, and I discovered mythology. But then we moved to a small town in order to enable my grandfather to realize his lifelong dream—raising thoroughbreds. It was culture shock. I was no longer weird—just a well-dressed outsider. I concentrated on academic hoops, jumping through them to continue to prove Mrs. B., Mrs. H., and Mrs. M. wrong. I spent lots of time rounding up our horses, who had magical abilities with gate latches, from other people's property. I also found Shakespeare—what a guy!

I'm always baffled when friends inform me of their contempt for William. I can't comprehend anyone not loving the person who wrote the most beautiful lines in English; Even, "She should have died hereafter. . . ," can thrill me when read or spoken. And how can Queen Margaret's speech from Richard III, "What were you snarling all before I came, ready to catch each other by the throat. . .," be described as anything less than magnificient? Finding Shakespeare was worth exile on the farm.

I want to get my master's in Reading and concentrate on helping prisoners of illiteracy achieve parole. ∎

5 | I Am a Writer

If you are not a writer, you will not understand the difficulties of writing.

Mem Fox

Teaching writing must be *about* writing. We cannot be like the tennis coaches who spend a week of instruction explaining how to hold a racquet before actually letting our students play the game. Writers write. They write daily for different purposes, for different audiences and with different outcomes. Some writing will make it to a final draft. Other writing will be discarded along the way, and yet it too teaches about writing achievement. Not all of our attempts need to be worthy of publication. Not all of our attempts represent the pinnacle of our writing. But in the trying lies the essence of the writer.

A portfolio allows for all of these ideas to come into play. The process of writing is valued and displayed, and a writer's range and depth can be exhibited in a portfolio. This chapter, while displaying range, cannot show depth without showing all the artifacts of one writer. Instead we chose to demonstrate the variety of writing possibilities.

Teachers of writing must write with their students. We write right along with ours. We demonstrate topic choice, genre choice, peer editing, author's chair, revision strategies, and publication possibilities as we write with our students on a daily basis. We want teachers to see the power of writing to create a community of writers. We feel we are each but one member of this writing community.

The following artifacts represent a variety of students' writing. The majority of our students initially do not consider themselves to be writers, but by the end of the semester this has changed for most of them. We feel we have years of poor writing teachers to overcome. Young adult author Chris Crutcher says that the hardest part of writing for him is silencing the voice that says, "Who the hell do you think you are?" This voice is still whispering in the ears of many of our students. We fear it is the voice of a former writing teacher. We hope that our students whisper more encouraging things in the ears of their students. It is to this end that we marvel at the amazing writing that they do. It's time for a different voice, and if you've never heard it before, how do you know how to provide it for someone else?

❚ This first-year teacher wrote a poem about staying alone in her house for the first time. She sees writing as therapeutic in nature and models different genres for her students frequently. This is but one example she included in her portfolio.

I was inspired to write the attached poem when I stayed in my house alone for the first time. I do not remember a time I have ever been alone overnight before this. I was very nervous about it. It took a lot of talking to my self to convince myself to finally fall asleep. But it was hard, with all those noises. You see, I live in an older house that still has radiators that heat it. When the boiler in the basement clicks on, it sounds like the pits of Hell have come to life. Thus came the inspiration for my poem. This was therapy for me to write this poem. It helped me to rationalize the bumps in the night and to finally fall asleep!

Boiler Vents in the Dark

It grumbled and groaned as it awoke in the cellar,
Shaking the walls in its path.
The whole house seemed alive and quaking.
It broke the seal of silence promised by the night,
With rattles like dry bones scrapping and strumming the walls.
My whole body trembled down to the roots of my soul.
Fear of the unknown hiding in the dark gripped my arm,

With ice cold fingers callused from too much use.
He was no stranger to my room.
My eyes strained and scanned about in expectation,
For the supernatural shadows to finally materialize.
My breath came in short tight gasps,
My heart pounded and screamed out the secret,
I lay still as if paralyzed in anxious anticipation,
Of the unknown I could not see ready to do its deed upon me.
I waited,
and I waited.
Every breath in expectation as though it were my last.
All was in despair again as the boiler clicked itself off,
Resting for the next attack on my sanity tomorrow night.
The stillness is almost unbearable now.
I wait breathless and nervous with every new second,
Ticking away timeless short-lived moments I have to encounter.
I still wait in prolonged expectation,
For the welcomed drowsy sleep I dream of,
Where I can escape the rantings and ravings,
From this mad old house. ▌

▌ This veteran teacher writes a lot with her students. She also models her process of writing with her students. In class Kathy mentioned that this particular day was the day in history when the pencil and eraser had been patented. That is all this teacher needed to hear—she was off writing poems about pencils! This teacher is a writer who can find ideas for writing everywhere. She is also an excellent role model for her students regarding writing strategies and responding to writing.

In class we heard about the patenting of the pencil and eraser. We also discussed a variety of poetry. I lay in bed that night and jotted down things that came to my mind about pencils. These poems were the result of those musings.

I shared these with my students and they loved them. I see I still need to revise the last free verse. In my mind, I made the connection it was the teacher's fault—she gave the quiz, thus the pencil was chewed upon. I need to make that clearer.

This was a good lesson for me as well as my students on the importance of response to writing!

The Old Pencil

There was an old pencil from Trifle
Who got shorter the longer his life
Until one day
He was eaten away
By the pencil sharpener he took as a wife.

The Pencil

Why oh why are people so cruel?
Thought the woeful pencil left alone after school.
My back aches so from a bite and a chew.
Don't students know we have feelings too.

But as he lay there in self-pity,
Up walked Miss Jennifer whom he thought was pretty.
"There you are!" she said with glee.
"I thought you were lost forever from me."

Confident and bold the pencil felt that night
As Jennifer had chosen him in order to write.
I'm glad I'm a pencil, I'm needed again
And he proudly placed a period at the end.

Pencil in Mourning

The grieving yellow pencil
Rubbed his teary eyes
And pondered his tormenting day.
Chewing
Biting
Gnawing
Within moments the eraser was gone.
The eraser,
Pencil's lighthearted friend,
Together
Since they were created.
But who's to blame? Who's to blame
For the eraser's ill-fate?
The anxious child taking a test?

Or perhaps
It was the teacher's fault. ▮

▮ This first-grade teacher used a children's book that was read in class (*Fun, No Fun* by James Stevenson) as a model for writing. In the book, James Stevenson reflects on what he thought was fun and no fun when he was growing up. This teacher saw that book as a perfect model for her own writing. She contrasted things she liked with things she didn't like in a format like that of the book. She models for her students that writing ideas can be borrowed from published books and authors.

After hearing the book Fun, No Fun *by James Stevenson in class tonight, I felt moved to write my own list of fun and no fun activities. I borrowed the format from James Stevenson, but made it my own by thinking about things in my own life that I like and don't like. I think children's literature can serve as a wonderful model for writing. Often when students say they don't have anything to write, I'll invite them to reread a favorite picture book and encourage them to write in a similar style to that writer. I like books like this one that invite readers to respond in writing with their own thoughts and ideas. Good books can't help but inspire writing in all of us.*

Fun	No Fun
Riding the Tilt-A-Whirl at the State Fair	Feeling sick afterward
Buying Christmas presents	Paying the bills
Folding clean laundry	Putting away the laundry
Being sick in bed for one day	Being too sick to enjoy it
Snow	Having to do errands in it
Going on vacation	Getting ready to go on vacation
Popcorn at the movies	The bottom of the popcorn bucket
Going to the beach	Cleaning sand out of your bathing suit
Having a writing idea come to you	Thinking about ideas to write about
Dreams	Nightmares
Clean sheets in the summer	Changing the sheets

New Year's	The end of February
Fireworks	Mosquitos
Picnics	Ants
Sunburn (a little)	Athlete's foot
Rain showers	Leaving the windows open when it rains
Classes	Tests
Grocery shopping	Putting groceries away
Writing with my favorite pen	Writing when I can't find my favorite pen
Ordering books	"Not available"
Baking	Cleaning up
Letters from a friend (best-packages!)	No mail
Finding more of whatever I just ran out of in the pantry	Having to run to the store in the middle of cooking
Stamps with pictures	Plain flag stamps
A crossed-off "To Do" list	A list I have to start over with tomorrow
The smell of lemon oil	The smell of a bathroom begging to be cleaned
Sleeping with the windows open	Sleeping with the air conditioner on
Finding $20 in the dresser drawer	Still having eight more days until payday
Legos	Lincoln logs
Skating	Bowling
Sour cherries, Tootsie Pops, M&M's	Orange slices, black jelly beans, circus peanuts
Gingerbread	Coconut
New crayons	Old crayons
Back to school	Midterm
Plastic-coated paper clips	Bulldog clips
Old photographs	Old photographs with no names or dates on the back
A listening ear	Advice ∎

❙ This nontraditional undergraduate student wrote her writing autobiography as a way to reflect upon her own writing. After talking about her own writing and writing instruction throughout her education, she makes writing plans. These writing plans are ideas she has for writing, which are very specific and important to her. I hope she models this selection of writing topics for her own students one day.

I have rewritten my writing autobiography here. Although the first version was very negative, it was therapeutic and a necessary step to this . . . my revised writing autobiography.

You may think I have bad feelings about myself as a writer, however, all my childhood memories served to reinforce the idea that I am a good and creative writer. My frustration stems from the difficulty I have in beginning a writing project. I procrastinate until the last possible moment and then I write and rewrite and rewrite.

Words have a rhythm and an order in my mind. If something feels out of beat, I can't let it go. Even now, if a friend asks for help on a note to parents or my husband asks for advice on a letter to clients, I rearrange words to find a pattern/beat that satisfies some innate sense in me.

Because writing is such a process to me, it has become less and less appealing. Amazingly, although processed writing takes me forever, what I have the most difficulty with is trying to journal a short 5–10 minute paragraph about some random idea. Without a purpose, I am at a loss for even a starting point.

Today, however, I have a purpose: my writing history. So, without further ado . . . (This is a segue.)

Chapter One: Grade School

My earliest memories of writing begin in grade shool. When I would write, I would use big words that were new to me. I loved to use adjectives, metaphors and similes. I would start by writing something like this: "It was a sunny day until the sky became cloudy." Next, I'd think and rewrite to something like this: "It was a sunny day when suddenly the storm clouds began to cover the sky like spots on a leopard." Finally, out would come the dictionary (we had no thesaurus) and I'd embellish: "The day was filled with brilliant sunlight when unexpectedly a tumultuous outburst of rain clouds began to speckle the sky like abundant spots on the back of a leopard."

Writing was like a game to me. I'd been reading all kinds of books and I liked to write in what seemed to be "flowery" writing. However, I was a perfectionist and even in grade school, I remember writing and rewriting. Because

I learned to depend so heavily on the dictionary, my written vocabulary has always greatly exceeded my oral vocabulary. Even now when I write, I have words in my head that I like and want to use. Therefore, I always have a dictionary nearby to make sure I use them correctly.

Fortunately, my 5th-grade teacher saved a story I wrote and presented it to me at my high school graduation. It is the only sample of my work that I have from when I was in grade school. At the time, it reinforced my confidence as a writer. Now, it reinforces my awe of Mrs. Josephine Lorenz as a teacher. The confidence she gave me be saving that single sheet of notebook paper for seven years, is something I hope to remember when I start teaching.

Chapter Two: Junior High School

In junior high, one of my teachers wanted to start a monthly school newspaper. She asked a friend and me to be co-editors. Our job was strictly creative and humorous writings; no "real" reporting. We did student interviews, such as, "If you were stranded on a desert island, what one thing would you want with you?" We interviewed three or four teachers each month, asking them each the same questions and then printing their responses. We also did tongue-in-cheek articles, making up stories based on inside-the-school humor. Occasionally we were censored, not for improper langauge, but because the humor was a little too cutting. This writing was fun. It also was a game. The night before a deadline, Shirley and I would be on the phone writing and rewriting our monthly editorial. Regrettably, I threw out all the copies of these newspapers a few years later while on a wild cleaning spree.

Chapter Three: High School

In high school I took three years of journalism. We had to choose between working on the school newspaper or the yearbook. I had a crush on a boy who dated the newspaper's editor. She had a great dislike for me, he didn't, and I chose the yearbook. Because of that choice, to this day I still can't put photos in a scrapbook and have them face off the page—a big yearbook no-no!

My senior year I was made editor of the yearbook. It wasn't something that I wanted to happen, it was kind of a natural progression. Unfortunately, I was extremely busy that year. I had become overly responsible to a number of clubs. The yearbook became more of a nagging chore than an expressive release. Deadlines and their responsibilities were overwhelming. I developed a love for the dark room where my friend Gaylene and I would go because when the red light was on, no one could come in. Mrs. Wagner would yell through the door but she couldn't enter. It was a haven.

Positive writing experiences that I had in high school include competing in the Nebraska State Journalism Contest and writing skits for pep rallies. At the State Journalism Contest, I competed in "theme or mood copy writing for yearbook" and placed second. I also wrote many parodies which we used for skits in pep rallies and Jobs Daughter fund-raisers. Some were based on songs, some on poems and some on popular commercials. This writing in particular, seemed to be my forte and I loved it.

Chapter 4: Adulthood (?)

My writing experiences now consist of lists, letters, notes, school assignments and thank-yous.

When I do serious writing, it still tend to get a little too flowery and sound like "mood" copy. As it was in my younger years, the things that I have been most successful with are creative compositions and parodies. I wrote a poem for the slide show dialogue at my mom and dad's 25th anniversary. I wrote skits based on various songs for my grandparents' 50th anniversary (in which all 25 of the grandchildren were forced to participate). I wrote a Christmas letter based on the Night Before Christmas. I wrote a birthday invitation (for a bus ride to the Nebraska game) in the shape of an N.

One major transition for me has been learning to create on a word processor. It's not as easy for me to edit while I type as it is while I write. Usually I type all my paper, print it out, edit it and make additional notes, then go back into the document and change it. My thoughts come randomly more than sequentially and I think that is why it has been such a transition for me. However, I am making progress.

Epilogue

To conclude my writing history I would like to focus on my writing future by listing some of the thoughts I want to express on paper:

I. Letters and stories for my children
    A. Their stories about their "love lives"
    B. Their stories about school incidences and bus rides
    C. Funny things that they say
    D. Moments I'm proud of them

       E. Moments when I hurt for them

II.   The story of my sister's near-fatal car crash

    A. The phone call

    B. My brother and me visiting her in rehab

    C. My feelings on the sentencing of the man who hit her

    D. Jan with a cane (the aftereffects)

III.   Stories from Granpa Hoggins

    A. Write the stories he taped on the cassette

    B. Stories he told me on the ride from Topeka

IV. A diary of the yearly Christmas get-together of me and ten of my high school friends

    A. New information

    B. Old favorite stories

    C. Bios on each of the girls: Sandy, Jan, Tammy, Lori, Dee, Vicki, Gaylene, Patty, Louise, Cindy

This will be a good start to launch me into future writings. That is the good thing about history . . . it makes us keenly aware of the future! ▮

▮ This first-year teacher included a poem in her portfolio. She wrote this poem when she was in high school and was very proud of it. What she was upset about was the response it got from her teacher. She gave her an "F" for the poem and told her that it couldn't possibly be her own. This new teacher remembers distinctly how it felt to have her writing discouraged. Hopefully, she will channel this anger into being a much more accepting teacher and responder to her own students' writing.

I wrote this poem when I was a sophomore in high school. I'll never forget the anxiety I felt when the teacher told us that our weekend homework assignment was to write a poem. I knew I couldn't do it! What did I have to write about? After talking with my mom, she gave me several suggestions to try. Well, after hours of writing and erasing I finally came up with my poem and boy was I proud of it! For the first time, I felt confident about my writing abilities. I couldn't wait for Monday morning to come because I was so anxious to turn my assignment in. It seemed like weeks passed before our papers were returned to us. Then the day finally came! I'll never forget the horror I experienced after my name was called and I quickly reached for my poem. All I could see was red! As I gained my composure, the grade and the words became clear. I received a big fat "F" because my teacher claimed that she had read this poem somewhere before. How could she have read a poem I wrote for my dad? As I look back, I can't believe I didn't stand up for myself. I wrote the poem and felt I deserved a good grade! I feel this experience as well as others contributed to my fear of writing. I believe this helped me become a better teacher because I have made an enormous effort never to make my students feel the way I did.

Freckles

I have a freckle on my nose
As plain as it can be
No matter what I do to it
It's there for you to see.
Make-up doesn't hide it.
Sunburn makes it worse.
Why oh why am I the one
To have this terrible curse.
I've come to the conclusion
That freckles aren't so bad.
For when I looked across the room
I saw my freckled dad! ▮

▮ The memory piece was written during free-writing in Teaching Reading/Language Arts Methods, an undergraduate course. The student who wrote it, a young man who had been hesitant to share his writing with the class, offered it during author's chair. We had been discussing chickens following the reading of a children's literature title, and suddenly we all began telling chicken stories. This student couldn't get the chicken theme out of his mind, and wrote this story during his free-write.

When he shared this piece in author's chair, he received such thunderous applause and laughter—the two responses he sought—that he shared his writing regularly thereafter. This chicken piece, though, was the first that brought him success with his audience. As he told me after class, "I was nervous about sharing my writing. I've never really written much, only what I had to."

Following this experience this student became known, after numerous poems, as the "poetry man." He continues in this capacity today in his position as an elementary school teacher. Teachers are always asking him to share his writing now, because they've heard he can tell a great story with his words.

I included this artifact because it reflects the risk-taking in my writing that I am working on. I understand how important it is for a student to try new things, especially in writing. I have attempted that with this artifact. I tried this memory piece after we discussed chickens in class today. I guess other people have chicken stories, too. When are we going to write that chicken stories book? Anyway, this memory piece is what I wrote during our class writing time. I know a lot of people were writing teaching philosophies, or some serious kind of thing, but I was trying something new. In addition to it representing my attempt at risk-taking, it also represents my favorite response to my writing. When I shared this piece during author's chair, everyone laughed, at the parts they were supposed to laugh at. That felt great! I also liked that you said it reminded you of Gary Paulsen. That felt wonderful. I'm going to read that title of his, Harris and Me, that you recommended. I guess I'm a good enough writer that I remind a writing teacher of a very famous, rich author. I guess this risk-taking stuff can really work out.

Mouse in the Out House

I remember one time when I was ten or eleven years old being at grandma's house. It must have been for some holiday or some family event because there was a lot of relatives around. It seemed like there was always a battle for things like food, places to sit, places to sleep, and of course the use of the bathroom.

Well, one day while all this hoopla was going on I found myself in an uncomfortable predicament. I was backed up and needless to say the line to the bathroom was too. There was no other option but to go where few had gone before, to the outhouse by the chicken coop. I dreaded it immensely, but nature was calling. There was no light, but you couldn't keep the door open for fear of someone seeing you. Worse yet, I always feared that if someone knew I was there they would come and lock me in.

I finally got the courage up to go in. I never imagined I would ever have to use it but the time had come. I managed to pry the door open with my foot just enough to get a little light in. As I was sitting there I could not figure out how my dad and grandpa could use this on a regular basis.

Well, while I was sitting there, listening to the chickens tending to their usual activities, I caught a glimpse of something in the light, or did I? Just then a big fat mouse the size of a small dog, ran across my lap. Pants down and all, I jumped up, practically pulling the door off of the hinges, burst out of that bathroom from hell, screaming bloody murder. Needless to say, all my cousins had to be in full view.

To this day, I still hear their evil laughs and snickers. Will they ever forget? I think not. To this day, I have never returned to that particular potty. ∎

∎ These two poems were written during free-writing in English/Language Arts Methods. The student who wrote them was a former newspaper reporter who returned to school to get his English/journalism teaching credential. He was comfortable with writing with a deadline, so as people around him groaned about what he could accomplish in ten minutes, he'd shrug and say, "You get used to it."

These poems are both based on what the student was experiencing, or had just experienced. The pollen poem was so popular his peers still refer to it. The distracted poem dealt with an auto accident the student had on the way to class. Both illustrate how much our lives can affect our writing, if we only allow it. If I had given him a specific writing prompt, he would not have felt invited to deliver two such delightful poems. When he shared these poems in author's chair, the response was instantaneous and thunderous. He kept writing; he kept sharing.

I'm putting a couple of works in progress in my portfolio. I wrote both of these in class during our writing time, so both are in draft format. I may work on them some more over time, or maybe not. Both of them received great reviews from our classmates, so I probably will work on them. I find myself noticing what I'm noticing now. I guess I always really have; I'm a writer, but now I'm conscious of probably having to write about what happens to me, so I'm really noticing. I guess I would agree with you that literate people notice things. I'm doing that. At first I thought everyone else would think I was weird because I pay attention to things they do not, but they were all seemingly quite impressed that I could do this writing in five minutes, or so. I think my pre-writing goes on all the time, and when I finally take the time to write it down it comes pretty quickly. This is why my first drafts are so messy. I just want it down on paper. I've been fussing with it in my head for so long that I want it down before I lose any of it. Like I said, I'll probably work more on them later.

81

❚ The previous reflection and artifact are from Sheri's son (eight at the time of this entry). Justin has always enjoyed drawing. He makes sense of the world through his illustrations, whether he is depicting the plot of a story for language arts, or drawing his favorite Sega game characters, as in this case. Additionally, he invents new characters and sends them to Sega. He is confident that he will design computer games someday.

This artifact and reflection are part of a portfolio he keeps at home. Occasionally, he'll tell favorite teachers about it, but less so now that he is in middle school. These artifacts reflect his spatial intelligence and his overwhelming desire to spend his free time drawing.

I included this artifact in my portfolio because my mom made me. Sometimes I draw before I write about something. Or I draw instead of writing about something. Or I draw while I write about something. I almost never draw after I write about something. These drawings came from my bedroom walls, which my mom says I should mention are covered with drawings I have done of action characters. ❚

❚ The following artifact and reflection were provided by a graduate student in Sheri's storytelling workshop. She brought me this piece of writing one day after class and asked me to read it because it would help me understand her better. I never recovered. After I read the writing, the student shared the story behind the piece. She told me her daughter had been killed in an auto accident. Without pause, she went on to say that she had written this particular piece for a class and the professor had hated it because of the way it made him feel. I thought this an arrogant response—especially considering the pain it represented for the student. She had really risked a great deal to share something so intimate and important in her writing, and to be told that it was "too surreal" by the professor was unacceptable.

This writing will be with me always, as will this student, who helped me see that her story was a vital part of how she viewed life. Without knowing this story, one couldn't know the student. How many other such stories do our students carry with them that we, as their teachers, never take the time to listen to? How can a pain as great as this not influence and color everything that occurs in the classroom, and in life? How could I understand that when we told stories about death and dying this student had a very personal and immediate response, unless I knew her story?

This student changed me. I had always believed that we need to listen to our students' stories, but I never realized before how essential it is. After reading this story,

I sat at my desk and sobbed. Then I ran home to hug my children. I still see this student, and am eternally grateful to her. I had wondered why there was a part of her that seemed standoffish, unapproachable. I'd fretted about not being able to reach her. With her writing, I changed my perceptions of her. I couldn't possibly know how she felt, but I could listen and learn.

In this writing, this student shared more than who she was as a writer, she shared who she was as a person. This interpretation of how she felt the night of her daughter's death is, indeed, a defining piece of writing.

I included this story because it is about what matters to me. I suppose it helps to define me. When I turned this story in to an English professor in the past, he said, "You don't have the right to make me feel this way." I thought that unfair. The story was my viewpoint of an event that really happened to me. This was how I felt. He didn't like the "surreal" aspects of the story. Let me tell you, it felt surreal.

Frankly, I was annoyed with his response. I should have ownership not only of the story, but of the event I write about. This story captures, for me, the essence of this event. I think it is some of my best writing. I certainly know that it is the most powerful and meaningful writing I have ever done. I feel certain that after reading this, you will know me better.

Dance with Death

Death scythes inevitably. A timepiece begins at birth and one day this timepiece ceases to tick. Death does not recognize age, status, or assets. Death can be planned or unplanned, abrupt or prolonged, painless or painful, and sometimes even bring relief. Death can alter the lives of people left behind, can make them stronger, weaker, or render no effect whatsoever. Death exists as an intimate stranger who invades all lives at one time or another. No one can elude the grasp of Death. I know, for I have danced my own macabre dance with Death.

The evening began very pleasantly. The temperature was in the mid forties, there was a gentle breeze, the stars were gleaming brightly overhead, and the leaves were just beginning to turn colors. Halloween decorations, carved jack-o-lanterns, black cats, wicked witches, scary ghosts and goblins could be perceived up and down the residential street from my perch upon my cool cement stoop. I sat there enjoying my solitude and watched the leaves silently tumble to the ground. A sudden piercing, pealing of the telephone shattered the stillness and startled me from my reverie. A portent of foreboding permeated my answering immediately. I answered the telephone and a dark, black shadow descended over the beauty of life.

The hospital loomed ahead like a dark brooding hulk, its windows emerging as giant sightless eyes, and its glass doors cool as ice, whispering open soundlessly. I entered this place where life versus death, happiness versus sadness weigh, wondering which way the scales of being would fall for me. The armored doctor, not in steel, but demeanor, informed me my child was dead. I heard a roaring in my ears like an ocean at full tide, a tightness in my chest like a twisting vise, and utter denial springing forth from my lips. I insisted on seeing with my own eyes what my mind could not possibly postulate, even if it meant dueling armed guards to accomplish this feat. At last, my challenge was met and I was on my way to greet the unknown.

As I stood outside the solid white door with my hand on the cold metal knob my throat felt as dry as sandpaper and I could hear my heartbeat hammering in my ears. I slowly turned the knob and from that point forward it seemed as though I was outside my body watching a strange drama unfolding before my disbelieving eyes. The first thing I noticed as I entered the room were a pair of feet, very unusual feet, perfectly square feet, ten toes all in a row, all the same size. As my eyes continued upward across a stiff white sheet I then noticed two small delicate hands covered with several vivid cuts and many smaller abrasions. My eyes resumed their journey onward to a respirator in the mouth attached with strips of heavy white adhesive tape and at last, the face. A deep purple and black gash across the bridge of the nose, a dull green cloth covering the left side, a foreign hand holding it in place, but, the right side was young, beautiful, and perfect. As I moved closer and picked up the small, still, cool hand I could hear a disembodied voice in the background commanding, "Don't touch the green cloth, don't attempt to remove the cloth—under any circumstances!" I closed my eyes, grasped the hand tighter, thought, "this isn't happening, it's a terrible nightmare and soon I will wake up"; however, it was all too real and the onset of many nightmares to come.

I left my child, or should I say the shell of my child, as my child no longer inhabited this world. I went to the location where the accident had occurred, where my child had been breathing only a short time before. A car, its side missing, its exterior battered, its rear end sitting in the street, sat off to one side. Policemen and a man taking photographs were there to record all evidence for the record. I stood off to one side, not getting too near, just staring at the remains of the car, wondering how this happened and why.

Time eases pain, memories represent life, but the perforation of my heart will abide with me forever. The Death of my child has been a supreme trial of endurance and will continue to be so. I always expected my children to out-live me, not to outlive them. But, sometimes this is not possible. Death scythes inevitably, indeed it most assuredly does. ▌

▌ This artifact and reflection were written during writing workshop in Teaching Reading/Language Arts for elementary majors. This particular student included this artifact in her portfolio section, "I Am a Writer."

As a class, we tried to celebrate spring by decorating the boring university classroom walls with poetry and writing about spring. This person's attempt is shared here.

I wrote this poem for our class display of poetry about the seasons. After I wrote this poem and put it up in our classroom, on a poorly drawn cricket, I may add, I had several people come up and compliment me on my writing. This felt really good. I can't remember the last time someone has liked what I've written. Or, maybe, I can't remember the last time my classmates read something I'd written. Usually only the teacher reads my writing. I want to be certain I provide this for my students. A forum for students to share their writing and to receive positive feedback has worked wonders for me. I imagine it would do the same for my future students.

I remember thinking this poem was pretty good when I wrote it, but I never expected others to think so. I feel like I could go write seven or eight more poems. Actually, I did. I went home after all those compliments in class and wrote poetry. Wow! What is happening to me as a writer? I'm writing, again.

Stealing Summer

The humidity hasn't
    left the air
The mist
      gladly
   Enters pristine lungs

The sky is
   Crimson
      With the sunset and
      Stained Orange
        with the simple
          streetlight

And I write to save it
   in time

She brings me Sirens
And crickets
Only hatched since
The fourth of July

Rain stagnates in the
           Beige cement under
                  bare feet
and on the leaves of
           fragile dusty miller
                  mosquitos overpopulate
     the
                  lush grasses
as the fireflies
     hide
                  away

a moment I stole

—or was it secretly given—

to me? ▌

▌ The following artifact and reflection were written by Sheri's nine-year-old daughter, Elizabeth. She sees her mother holding writing group meetings and portfolio discussions. With no prompting from her mother, other than modeling, she has decided to create her own portfolio of her writing. She has divided it into "poems," "stories," "response to literature," and "graphs & charts"—a section that contains her garden journal, an idea she heard a reading master's student share in a portfolio session.

This particular poem comes from her poetry section. She has recently enjoyed using clip art for some of her poems, and this is one of those poems.

This poem is one of the first I wrote when I started my portfolio. It is pretty good, but I'm better now. I think writing takes practice, or as I always say: pencilling makes perfect! I write a lot of my things with a pencil first, so I can cross out in later drafts. This is a final draft of a poem about how impossible it is to be perfect, so we'd better stop trying. The only people who are perfect are in our dreams. No one is perfect and so we should just like who we are, and like our friends for who they are.

The one for me

Lizzie's too skinny,
Lauren's too fat,
Leslie's too serious,
Lindy's a rat,
I like Erin
and she likes me a great deal,
The only thing I wish

is that Erin were real.

❙ This artifact is from Kathy's portfolio. I have a four-year-old son who is beginning to write in letterlike forms. He and I have been keeping a daily journal. Usually he has me write what he remembers from his day and then he draws a picture to go with it. I wanted to include something from this daily writing in my portfolio.

My four-year-old son and I write daily in our journals. Usually I write for him and he draws the pictures. But on this day, he wanted to draw his bear and he wanted me to tell him how to write bear. *I modeled this for him and then he practiced the letters and other letters he knew how to write. I included this in my portfolio to show the importance of parent modeling and of a parent providing the outlet for daily writing and drawing. The journal is something he thoroughly enjoys writing/drawing in. He often "rereads" previous pages and tells me what they say and describes his drawings. I am confident that he will continue to develop as a writer.* ❙

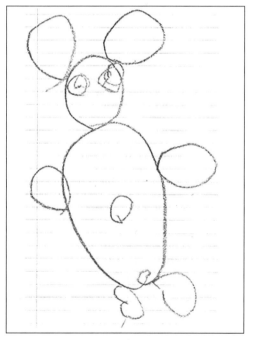

❙ This artifact is from Kathy's portfolio. I write with and for my four-year-old son, modeling the process. I think this is an important role for a parent or a teacher, showing the lifelong aspect of writing.

My son was obssessed with balls when he was about three years old. He would find balls everywhere—in the sky (the moon), in candy stores, etc. I wrote a picture book manuscript because of his interest in balls and submitted it to a number of children's book publishers. After countless form letter rejections, I made my own book for my son, complete with illustrations. He loves it! Even though no one else wanted it, my son appreciates it.

I included this in my portfolio for a number of reasons. First, it shows where I get writing ideas (my son is a rich resource for ideas). Second, it shows that I tried to get something published. And third, and most important, it shows that writing for an audience is important. Having something published in the form of a book is not the reason I write. I write because I love to write and I always will. My son loves to read my writing and to me, he's the most important audience I have.

I can't ask my students to write if I don't write too, struggling with the process of making sense and meaning while paying attention to a real audience for my writing.

The Moon Is a Ball in the Sky

The moon is a ball in the sky.
A cherry is a ball in a pie.
A pea is a ball in a pod.
A bobber is a ball on a rod.
An egg is a ball beneath a bird.
An o is a ball in a word.
A lollipop is a ball on a stick.
A candle is a ball with a wick.
A pillow is a ball on a cot.
Ice cream is a ball when it's hot.
Some yarn is a ball for a cat.
A pom pom is a ball on a hat.
The earth is a ball out in space.
Two eyes are balls on a face.
A balloon is a ball for a friend.
And a period is a ball at THE END. ∎

6

I Am a Listener

If for one minute I think I am better than someone, I won't hear what that person has to say.   Donald Graves

We included the artifacts in this chapter because they show the importance of being a listener. Listening has many purposes. Beyond listening for information, listening can also move students to write, to read, to connect, to speak, and to listen again more carefully. If we truly believe in the importance of establishing a community of learners, how else can we begin but by listening?

Listening is a form of reflection. By seeking to understand what another person is saying, a listener can't help but pause and consider his or her own point of view within the context of the speaker's story. We need to pause and ask ourselves as well as our students, How do I show that I am listening carefully?

Teachers must model the process of listening and help students develop strategies for improving their own listening. The very notion of respecting others starts with listening. We cannot respect differences, or learn from each other, if we don't hear each other's stories.

❙ This nontraditional undergraduate student had been working with Title I students before taking this class. She speaks in her reflection piece about the importance of listening to children. Her artifact describes her reaction to a class speaker who came to talk about classroom management. Again, this student related this topic to her own recent experience with Title I students.

About a year ago I was teaching a Title I program and had four kindergarten children. They had been coming for about two weeks when the speech teacher stopped me in the hallway. She wanted to know how many times I had noticed the speech problem of one of my students. I was truly embarrassed to realize that I hadn't even noticed that the little girl had a speech problem. I call this my great listening lesson. I had been talking so much that the children hadn't had a chance to express themselves and I hadn't given myself the opportunity to observe them.

As a teacher, I believe listening is more important than speaking. So much academic and personal information can be gleaned from the simple act of paying attention. Children have a great deal to offer and are not always given the opportunity to express their thoughts.

I know that I will need to model good listening habits for my students. As a community of learners, we gain insight, new ideas, and inspiration by listening to each other.

Myself As a Listener

On December 15, Mary Garland, a sixth-grade teacher, spoke to our class about classroom managment. I chose this particular presentation and discussion to write about because I believe that this is one of the most important skills that a teacher needs to acquire. It is also the one for which I do not feel prepared.

Mary first spoke about how there are not single answers to classroom management and that teachers need to find their own style. She explained three theories of discipline to us. The interventionist approach adheres to strict adult authority models including direct commands and consequences for breaking the rules. The noninterventionist focuses on child development and helping the student understand what is behind their behavior so that they can change it. The interactionist approach aims to develop a democratic environment and includes peer leadership, choices, contracts and problem solving. Mary urged us to examine these approaches and determine which one or combinations of these approaches would work for us.

Mary spoke about the increasing numbers of at-risk students, particularly in the inner-city schools. She talked about the rationale for teaching life skills in the elementary classroom and she pointed out the procedures used for teaching these skills. She then passed around a list she is compiling of literature pertaining to the various life skills.

The third topic of Mary's presentation involved procedure and routine. She quoted Harry K. Wong who contends that the main problem in classrooms is not discipline, but the lack of procedures and routines. Mary defined procedure and routine and then described a three-step process for establishing both in the classroom.

I was absorbed in Mary's presentation and found that I was able to put some of the information to immediate use in my Title I classroom.

I am not sure which of the discipline philosophies I will end up adopting and adapting to my own classroom. Right now I am practicing some aspects of each in my Title I classroom. Last year I found that it was impossible to get anything done without a good amount of the interventionist approach. I also do a great deal of active listening and provide as many choices as I can. I also try to use positive, honest reinforcement much more often than punishment.

I was disturbed by Mary's information about the increase in at-risk students, even though this is not new to me. I know that many people feel that teachers should not have to teach life skills and that it takes away from academic time. I feel that we really have no choice, because many children are just not coming to school with the social skills that they need. I was glad to see exactly how these skills are taught and that it really doesn't have to take a lot of time away from other pursuits. Mary also added many ideas for integrating these skills into the rest of the school day.

Mary's information about routine and procedure was by far the most helpful in the immediate sense. I have been experiencing a lot of chaos in my Title I classes every time the groups of students entered and left the room. I couldn't believe that I hadn't thought about establishing procedures for coming into and going out of the room. I went to work that same day and established a few simple procedures. It's made a tremendous difference in how I feel and in how the students behave. Mary gave us copies of a procedure and routines checklist and it feels as if I own a piece of gold. I know it will give me a good start in my first teaching job.

This presentation gave me a lot of useful information and the reassurance that there are workshops and help available for teachers. I am convinced, after this experience, that every education student needs a course in classroom managment. ▮

▌This author is a first-year teacher in our college's CADRE (Career Advancement and Development for Recruits and Experienced Teachers) program. This is a group of first-year teachers who are working on their master's degree. This cohort group is very close. They work together, have classes together, and generally rely on one another for support. This teacher wrote about one class session in which she responded to what was said and how she related to all of it. She asks some important questions in her reflection piece about the students in her own class and how she can help to enhance their listening. The CADRE program has built in a community of learners for these teachers, making listening and learning as natural as talking to and with one another.

Myself as a Listener

In this section, I have included a piece on listening to a class discussion. At first, I thought that all I could say about the "so what?" was that it is required for this portfolio. The more I thought about it, though, I realized that there was more to it.

From responding to this particular class session, and the various discussions that took place, I got to thinking about how I listen. I realized that I pretty much had a series of thoughts related to everything that was discussed in class that night. First of all, that told me that I was obviously listening, otherwise I wouldn't have had any response. Second, it made me realize that I really do tend to relate everything that I hear to my life, opinions, and experiences. Is that a little too egocentric? Or is that a sign of "actively" listening? Or is it just a result of everything in the class actually having something to do with me, since I am a member of it? I'm assuming that that's probably the case. It probably also helps a lot that what is discussed in class is meaningful to me. I highly doubt that I would be able to recall as much about a class discussion about World War I. (I know I don't have a clue today about what I learned about it in the past!) Anyhow, I have to wonder what my students listen to and actually hear in my classroom. Do the things I teach mean something to them? Do they have enough experiences to relate the subject matter to? I'll have to keep that in mind.

Response to Class Discussion on November 29

Class began with Tobi giving her book sharing. She read *Just a Dream* by Chris Van Allsburg. She began her book sharing by passing around gum to all of us. What a wonderful way to intrigue an audience, especially kids! She then read the book to us and shared some of her ideas and books related to ecology.

I learned that Tobi has an extremely pleasant reading voice. She is very soft-spoken while reading, as she is during conversations. It made me think about how I read and speak. I realized that I am much louder and probably do not sound as pleasant as she does when I speak. Her book sharing also made me think about my habits regarding ecology. I do not make much of an effort to recycle, except for aluminum cans. I am much like Walter was in the beginning. I am in too much of a hurry and too busy to take the time to sort out my trash.

Susan also gave her book sharing. She read *Who's in the Shed?* by B. Parkes. I'd never seen that book before. It was about farm animals, which was a good book for first graders since they study farms.

During her book sharing, I thought about the way she read the story, and how I would read it. I realized that I would read it differently. If I were to read it, I would place accents in different parts of the sentences. I began thinking about different reading and teaching styles. I wondered what it would be like to observe other CADRE teachers while they read aloud to their classes. I bet it would be really interesting to compare how differently we would read to our students.

Kathy discussed our portfolios. She shared some of her work with us and talked about some of the requirements. She told us that she had a table of contents in her portfolio. I realized that that was a good idea and took note of it so that I remember to add it to my portfolio. She also talked about the self-assessment portion of the portfolio, and shared her piece with us. She told us to look at the rubric in our packets since that is what she uses for assessment. From this I learned that is would be in my best interest to look that over before handing in my portfolio.

Kathy also gave us some questions to think about for our portfolio conference with her. I learned that I need to do some thinking about the contents of my portfolio before my conference.

We discussed reader response theory and jotted down a few names of people who have different theories. I learned that I agree with Louise Rosenblatt. I also believe that reading is an interactive process between the reader, writer, and the text. I do not feel that we must discuss or write about the books we read. Personally, I read books simply for the enjoyment that I get from reading. Yet, I do include discussion and writing in my teaching in order to meet the varying needs of the children in my classroom.

We also discussed grammar and talked about Ruth Heller's books on parts of speech. We then did an activity about adjectives, using candy. I learned a great way to excite students about learning adjectives. I know my students would really get into this activity! Food is definitely a great way to reach my kids.

Sheri Rogers came into class and talked a little about what her class in the spring is going to be like. I learned about the format for the course. Since we will only be meeting as a whole class a few times, I realized that our CADRE won't be together very much in the spring. This led to a conversation after class when several of us went out to dinner. This semester we've met after class on Wednesdays and before class on Thursdays. We are wondering when we're going to get together next semester. Both of our classes will only be meeting a few times. We decided that we will need to figure out a new schedule for going out to dinner. We agreed that we need to continue meeting on a weekly basis in order to keep our sanity! Our social gatherings this semester have been a wonderful opportunity for us to share experiences and to help us realize that we're not alone in our frustrations. ∎

∎ This first-year teacher is also a member of the CADRE program. She teaches high school English and has included a listening journal for one week as her artifact. She talks about the importance of listening, especially for teachers.

Myself as a Listener

I think one of the most difficult things in the world to do is listen to people when they are talking. I think it takes great skill to be a good listener, and many times I think people are too concerned with themselves to take the time to be a good listener. I don't know that this is done on purpose as much as it is a person's vanity to hear themselves talk. Let's face it, we all like to hear ourselves speak, and I think people don't always realize that many times others just want us to be quiet, listen, and not say a word. I know I have often longed for someone to just nod their head and listen to me talk because I was trying to work it out within myself, but needed someone to be there to talk to.

I love listening to people mainly because I feel I can learn a lot when I listen to them, but also because it is so interesting. I included a listening journal which I kept for five days because it shows how amusing it can be to just sit back and listen to people and not say a word.

I think I am a good listener partly because I can sense when people just want me to listen and just get something off their chest. I try hard to be an active listener by sometimes repeating something a person says back to them in my own words. I try very hard not to offer advice unless I have been specifically asked to do so, and I try to ask them questions about what they are talking about in order to show them I am interested in what they are saying. For example, one of my students came to class upset and asked to go to the bathroom. I told her to go and take her time. When she came in her eyes were red and I just walked out the door with her and she just sobbed because she was having a bad day. I just stayed back and let her cry until she was able to talk and then I listened to her tell about why she was crying. I did not pry her for information, nor did I tell her to just forget it and things would be fine tomorrow. I just listened to her until she was starting to look better, and then we talked about some other things.

I feel that listening is imperative as a teacher, but I also know that it can be difficult to do especially when students are giving you feedback about something. I try to ask for feedback, but believe me, I do not like it if it is negative. It is hard to stand back while someone criticizes me. I guess I know now how my students must feel sometimes.

Listening Journal

I decided to keep a listening journal and reflect on the different things I hear each day. I think it is fun to listen to people when they are talking, but not in a nosy sort of way. Sometimes people are so close to you that you just can't help hear what they are saying. In addition, it is more interesting when you walk into the middle of an ongoing situation and you hear part of the story and it sounds even more outrageous then it really is. I especially like it when my students are doing a group project in which they are able to talk to one another while they are working. The things they say to each other are hilarious, and usually they have no idea that I can hear pretty much every word they say. Here is my listening journal for five days in an average school week.

Monday, October 30:

This morning I was by two colleagues who were talking about a situation with which I am somewhat familar with. It involves a student and a teacher, so naturally it is a touchy situation. They began whispering, but since I was so close I could still hear them talking. This always makes me feel uncomfortable because I wonder if they think I am trying to listen in on their conversation. It made me feel uneasy, so I left the area until they were finished speaking with each other. What a tough job listening can be!

I think the best people in the world to listen to are teenagers. They are so much fun when they are talking to each other because they are so honest with one another. I also feel they have a lot of insight about life in general.

I listened to a group of boys in my sixth hour who never tire of talking. They are especially funny when they talk one on one with each other. They get pretty open and usally start teasing one another. They called one boy "Master Nord" in a sarcastic manner because he told them an answer to something then it turned out to be wrong. Since it is mostly guys in this room they get pretty sarcastic with each other, but in a fun sort of way. "Master Nord" was kind of an oxymoron to them.

Tuesday, October 31:

My students were doing a group project and talking quietly about different things. I was working at my desk and I'm always attentive as to what is going on in the class. The kids usually have no idea that I am listening to almost every word they say. Not that I'm going out of my way, but sometimes they are not very discreet about what they say to one another. Sometimes I'll acknowledge something they say or answer a question they've asked a friend, and they are shocked that I can hear what they say. I tell them that I have super-human hearing.

One boy came up to my desk to talk to me about the assignment and we talked a little more about other things and he looked at me and said, "Boy, you must hear a lot of different stuff up here. You must hear everything." I laughed because he was exactly right. He commented that if the other students knew what I could hear they may be embarrassed. One girl made a comment in reference to a question they had to answer about what they would want or need if they were stranded on a deserted island. She remarked that she would want Joe. Well all of the guys started whooping and hollering and teased her. It wasn't exactly what she meant, but it was too late. I don't think they let her forget what she said for about two or three days.

Wednesday, November 1:

I listened to a group of boys again today. Joe and Jason were arguing over the issue of hunting and whether or not it was right or wrong. Joe and Jason are not strangers to arguing because they do it almost every day. The funny thing is, they are really good friends. Joe will always resort to personal attacks when he argues and he will get really loud and try to be over-powering. Sometimes it bothers me because Jason tends to follow Joe blindly.

The two boys argued about hunting and they were going back and forth and it was just hilarious listening to them. At one point Joe tried to tell Jason that his fishing and killing a fish were the same as Joe shooting a deer. Jason said no, "it's not like I am throwing a fish in a barrel and shooting it." I started laughing because I got this picture of someone throwing a fish into a barrel and shooting it. Well, then I couldn't resist, so I threw a question at them which I knew would set them off, and sure enough they took the argument to the next level. These guys always make the class very interesting.

Thursday, November 2:

Today, I listened to one of my students make a phone call to his mother. He asked to borrow a phone in the office area, so he was not too far away from my desk. Bryan called his mother from school and asked her to take out the pop he had left in the freezer. He said he didn't want it to explode. It was just kind of funny listening to the phone conversation from my point of view. I looked at him when he asked her the question, and he got this cute smile on his face. Bryan is a nice young man.

In my third-period class, I listened to two students have a conversation about religion. I guess the story behind this conversation began the other day when a boy who was near my student, Jeremy, said that all people who don't believe in Jesus are going to go to hell. Well, Jeremy is Jewish, so naturally he was upset by the comment. Another student in our class, Erin, tried to reassure him that not all people who are Christians believe that. However, it did not make Jeremy feel any better. I was saddened by the the whole conversation because I knew Jeremy was mad at the comment, and I knew I couldn't really say anything to make him feel better. Sometimes people need to be more careful when they make stupid remarks.

Later that evening, while in research class, Angie said something that was hilarious. She raised her hand and made a statement, which was supposed to be a question to the professor. It went something like this: "So basically we don't have to worry about bombing this class because you are going to help us all by giving us an 'A'." I don't think that was exactly what she meant, but the whole class roared.

Friday, November 3:

Today I had an interesting conversation with my students. I listened to it very carefully because we have not been getting along with one another lately. The problem is they are reading a novel and they feel they are having to read too much at night. Well, normally I will always listen to my students' concerns and adjust the assignments if it seems necessary. But this time I am having a hard time doing that. I did listen to them though, and I thought carefully about their concerns, which sounded more like complaints, and reassessed my lesson plans. However, I really don't think the reading is too lengthy. I even asked another teacher what she did when she taught the novel, and I am right on task with what she did. ❙

▍These artifacts and the reflection piece were written by Sheri following a methods section of the Teaching of Reading/Language Arts, undergraduate session. In the course of this semester we have a practicum with sixth-grade students, and modeling listening to students always calls for me, I believe, to know what their interests are, so I take notes. I take notes at practicum on interactions between my students and the sixth-grade students, I take notes of students' interests and then share those with my students, and I take notes during class sessions when my undergraduate students share their thoughts about class readings, practicum, portfolios, learning, etc. Two methods students' thoughts about portfolios, and one page of my notes from an initial sixth-grade practicum session, are illustrated here.

I included these artifacts to illustrate a vital part of my personal philosophy of teaching: I listen to my students. I believe that of all the language arts, listening is the one most ignored in instructional time. In order to model its importance to my students, I take notes, constantly, of class sessions. I want them to not only SEE me writing down what they are saying, but also to HEAR me refer back to something they have said in conversation and WATCH me make the connections between their comment and our reading, our writing, and/or something someone else in our community has said. I want my students to do the same with their students. How could I possibly expect them to do so, if I don't model it for them on a daily basis?

In addition to one page of notes from a regular class day, I've also included two of my favorite quotations from former students of mine. I make certain that I share with students every semester something fabulous a student of mine said last semester. Delightful comments and quotations come not only from reading, they also come from listening to the wonderful contributions of the people around us. We only have to listen, and I am a listener.

> "I put a lot of myself in this portfolio. I'm proud of how it turned out. One very important thing I have learned in this class is that I am a writer. I want to write every day because it feels so good after you do it. It is like there is a relationship between me and my pen. No one else even has to read it. But it feels good that you do."
>
> *Methods Student*

> "I really mean it when I say that I have never done something for a class that meant as much to me as this portfolio. Everything in here is me, meaningful to me, and represents my growth as a learner. I cannot say here what I have learned this semester. I could not express it in 10 pages; it is invaluable. But a summary of it is this portfolio and I will carry it with me always."
>
> *Methods Student*

Brett — Hockey

Mortal Combat Audrick — video games, magazine

Nadia — gymnastics, art, swim — dance

Zack — art & archotical

Brunetta — dance, computer

Tyana — read & listen mysteries to music

Chris — art, 4 square video games read mysteries & fiction

Jessica — read & go shopping

Andrew — most sports (soccer state) read = SciFi

7 | I Am a Speaker

I know intellectually that language is an interactive, social process, but I'm only beginning to understand what that means emotionally. My writing, I'm realizing, nearly always has the socially interactive purpose of either creating relationships or ensuring that established relationships continue. Mem Fox

We include these artifacts because they illustrate the importance of the learner as a speaker. When students feel comfortable speaking in a classroom, they learn from and with each other. The teacher who models not only her willingness and ability to speak but also her ability and desire to listen to the student speaker allows for a community of learners to thrive and prosper in the classroom. If the teacher is the only speaker in the classroom, how can she possibly know her students?

The following artifacts examine the numerous meanings "I Am a Speaker" has for individual learners.

❙ On the first day of class, this nontraditional student introduced herself as a person who ate goldfish. I didn't know how to react to this! I thought maybe she was kidding, but I found out she wasn't. For her learning demonstration in class, she demonstrated how to eat goldfish. And then she did! She ate two goldfish right before our very eyes!

Needless to say, she had captivated her audience! We learned a lot about setting a table and about manners—as well as how to eat a goldfish.

In this section I have included my demonstration on eating goldfish. The importance of sharing who we are as a speaker is a crucial element to being a teacher. Even a teacher who has filled her curriculum with hands-on activities needs to be a speaker throughout the day to her students.

As teachers, when we speak to students it is important not to be inhibited and unresponsive. To be effective teachers we need to be enthusiastic and passionate about our lessons and the material being presented. Students will become bored and uninvolved if we are not resourceful and inventive.

I am not the best public speaker. Becoming a more articulate speaker is one of my goals. I did want to demonstrate, however, that even though I am lacking in some speaking skills, that I am still an energetic speaker with some enterprising ideas. I am not afraid to try and excite students and energize them with whatever it takes.

With the youth of today and their need for attention and their desire to be entertained, to be a truly effective teacher, it is essential to exhibit a zest for life. Sometimes when a teacher presents books and other learning materials to students, there is a need to dramatize or act-out part of the lesson. If a person is inhibited or embarrassed to act a little silly, they will not be able to present the material in the best way.

This was more than a demonstration on eating goldfish. It was more of an illustration of my personality. It was my way of showing that I plan on being an energetic teacher with some inventive and resourceful teaching methods.

When we originally discussed doing a storytelling or a demonstration, I wanted to do something fun and thought about the goldfish demonstration. When the other students began to tell their stories, I decided to change my idea and tell a story also. But, as time progressed, and almost everyone was telling a story, and most were using stuffed animals, I decided to go back to my original idea. It wasn't a great idea, but it was different and changed the pace in the classroom a little bit.

If I were really doing a demonstration for a classroom of students, I would probably alter the demonstration, depending on the age of the students. The goldfish could easily be exchanged for another "unusual" food that students would find similarly revolting. The point is, that there are a lot of books that are written pertaining to various aspects of food. Some of the books are outrageous, but sometimes that makes them more interesting to some students.

Food can be a very popular theme with students. Some of the activities I thought of to accompany the demonstration would really be worthwhile activities that most students would enjoy. They would be good learning experiences that were also fun. My own son did a class recipe book where every student demonstrated a recipe. The students had to write their own recipe, practice, and then demonstrate it for the class. He came home every night and wanted to re-create what had happened at school. His enthusiasm for the project was tremendous. Other parents told me similar stories about their children. My point is that food is usually a big hit with students, consequently, it can be incorporated into many learning experiences.

Goldfish or Other "Unusual" Food Eating Demonstration

Procedure

Before the actual eating occurs, illustrate how to set a table in the "proper" fashion. Also, you could have several lessons on proper table etiquette, and manners in general.

Inform the class about the "unusual" food you will be eating. If you use a goldfish, show the best way to catch and hold the fish while trying to eat it. Make sure you swallow the fish whole, it's hard to get the pieces out of your teeth. NOTE: You must buy "Feeder Goldfish."

Related Activities

1. Brainstorm appropriate etiquette and good manners. Have the students categorize them into priority lists. The students could write different vignettes showing good and bad manners and then perform them for the class.

2. Students could read about the history of manners and how certain customs developed. Students could research and investigate the story behind the origination of certain foods or eating items. For example, forks, spoons, or pitchers. Students could then create their own "new manner" or specific procedure that they have invented and write about it. Or, they could create some new utensil or similar item that could be used when eating a particular food.

3. Students could plan their own class party. They would need to discuss all the aspects of what it takes to have a party. They could write "To Do Lists," supplies required, procedures for games to be played, refreshment menus, and a variety of other things required for a particular party. They could also write invitations and thank you notes.

4. Read books about unusual foods and food combinations. Have the students write about their most unusual eating combination and how they happened to try it. Or, they could write about the most unusual one they have seen eaten and the circumstances surrounding it. They could also write and illustrate their own unusual food combination book as a class.

5. Students could read about and investigate different foods and share the most interesting facts found. They could do this by writing the fact on a strip of paper for a pocket chart and the students would have to match the fact with the particular food. You could finish by having a tasting party with different familiar foods and have the students match the food to its name. For example, kiwi, rutabaga, artichoke, or other unfamiliar foods. A survey could be taken to decide what was unknown to the children.

6. Research different foods in other cultures and countries. Students could keep a journal for a week with all the foods they have eaten and then try to match each one with the country of its origin. They could discuss their results with the class and share information to help other students complete their journals.

7. Students could demonstrate some activity, skill, or hobby that they are interested in, showing step-by-step procedures. They could then collect all of them and make their own class "How To Books." Another similar idea is to have students write down their favorite recipe and share it with the class. They could then make a "Class Recipe Book."

Related Books

Aliki. 1990. *Manners*. New York: Greenwillow Books.

Baruth, Philip. 1988. *Holiday cooking around the world*. Minneapolis: Learner Publications.

Brown, Marc, and Stephen Krensky. 1983. *Perfect pigs: An introduction to manners*. Boston: Little, Brown.

Carlson, Dale, and Dan Fitzgibbon. 1983. *Manners that matter for people under 21*. New York: E.P. Dutton.

Dahl, Roald. 1994. *Roald Dahl's revolting recipes*. Illus. Quentin Blake. New York: Viking.

Giblin, James Cross. 1987. *From hand to mouth or, how we invented knives, forks, spoons, and chopsticks and the table manners to go with them*. New York: Thomas Crowell.

Katzen, Mollie, and Ann Henderson. 1992. *Pretend soup and other real recipes: A cookbook for preschoolers and up*. Berkeley: Tricycle Press.

Parish, Peggy. 1978. *Mind your manners*. Illus. Marylin Hafner. New York: Greenwillow Books.

Penner, Lucille Recht. 1991. *Eating the plates: A pilgrim book of food and manners*. New York: Macmillan.

Perl, Lila. 1975. *Slumps, grunts and snickerdoodles: What Colonial America ate and why*. Illus. Richard Cuffari. New York: Clarion.

Shapiro, Rebecca. 1962. *Wide world cookbook*. Boston: Little, Brown.

Stubis, Patricia, and Talivaldis. 1975. *Sandwichery: recipes, riddles, and funny facts about food*. New York: Parents' Magazine Press.

Wilkes, Angela. 1994. *The children's step-by-step cookbook: Photographic cooking lessons for young chefs*. New York: Dorling Kindersley. ▌

▌ This student was a first-year teacher who found herself teaching in an inner-city school. She did not have much experience working with students of diverse culture prior to this. The artifact that she collected and reflected upon shows how she has learned from her students.

My classroom is made up of twenty very special and unique individuals. I have an ethnically diverse classroom. All students (African American, Hispanic, Asian American, and Anglo) speak a language of their own. I found myself unable to understand my students and so I shared with them that when I was in sixth grade the cool way to talk was "Valley Girl Talk." I demonstrated this language for them, much to their amusement. I also stressed that it was important for me to learn a standard English—the language of power. I related that I, too, did not speak this way every day or in every situation, or with every group of people I came in contact with. My language choices changed, depending on with whom I was speaking or writing. I learned to speak a standard English in school to help me be successful in academics. I was grateful for the opportunity to practice this type of language because it was not always appropriate to use this language in other social situations. Together, my students and I came to an agreement about language use in the classroom. We agreed that this was our practice ground for using a standard English. With this in mind, my students and I have learned about when it is appropriate to make different language choices. Audience consideration is important to my students now because we have talked about the importance of language settings. In this way I have been a speaker model for my students.

Slang Journal
Courtesy of my sixth graders

In hearing all of the "street talk," I was interested to discover what it was these young people were talking about. My students were gracious enough to help me understand. Together we compiled a list of popular slang terms. This project was very interesting and amusing to pursue. I believe that it was enjoyed by all. It was by me because it allowed me to talk with my students in a different way, where they were the teachers to me. I enjoy every opportunity I have to learn from my students. I know after this activity, students today know a lot more about life than I ever did in sixth grade.

This is the result of our project. This would not have been possible for me without their help. I would like to give them credit for this. Thank you: Maurtice, Ebony, Lindsay, April, Rachel, Jasmyne, Brandon, Crystal, Lester, Marlon, Dwain, Tierra, Jennifer, Michael, Nickie, Brett, Erich, Leonarda, Joi, and Ashlei.

stack-o-la saving up money

tight means something nice looking

baggin this is when you are making fun of someone

homie a good friend

hood rat a hoodlum or a bad kid

Bebe's Kid you are really bad or evil

buggin getting on your nerves

Mark this is a name you are called when you are in the wrong

dissin me this is when you want someone to stop putting you down

pimp walk this is the cool way to walk to show you are a gangster. You walk slowly and with a sort of smooth limp.

brick wall means be quiet. This is also a gesture where an opened hand is put very close to the face of the person you want to be quiet.

key locks this is a term used when you see a nice car

dap means that you agree and that you are right

all that means that you think that you are very cool and special

trippin means that someone is getting on your nerves

played out means that something is dated or is old news

get wit choo means that you are going out with someone

hook up means that you like someone and would like to go out with them *word up* means that you are speaking the truth

check yourself means that you need to take a step back and see what your problem is. A synonym also for this saying is the word recognize.

you go girl is a saying that means something like more power to you

bump that means forget about it

down low means that you need to be quiet

kicks another term for tennis shoes

heads up going to get in a fight

strip joint place where stolen cars are brought to be stripped

jacked up you have evidence of a fight on your face, bruises and cuts, etc.

yeh ya is a term for money

ged up means that you are dressed up nicely

lope this is another term for a friend or a "dude"

hoochie means that you dress to attract the opposite sex on purpose

phat means that something is nice looking. A synonym would be "tight." ▌

▌ This student was a first-year teacher who worked in a children's bookstore. For her book sharing presentation, she selected a book about Halloween and prepared a list of many related books. She read the book to other teachers with much expression and enthusiasm and received some hearty applause after her presentation. This caused her to reflect on the importance of reading with expression.

Myself as a Speaker
In this section, I have included my handout for my book sharing. I read The Vanishing Pumpkin *by Tony Johnston to the class. I chose to share this book because I really enjoy reading it to children. I first read it aloud to the kindergarten class that I student taught last year. I was amazed that the children applauded after I read it. I don't really know if it was the*

story itself that they applauded, or if it was the way I read it. I hope it was a little of both. I try to read with a lot of expression and voice inflections in order to show my enthusiasm for the books I read. I don't believe that there is any point in reading aloud to an audience if you don't put any energy or enthusiasm into it. I believe that good books can bore children (or adults) to tears if they are not read well. I feel that it is extremely important to do everything you can to entertain your audience, whether you're reading a picture book or teaching addition facts. I know that I pay much more attention to people when their tone of voice is appealing, rather than monotone. Therefore, I always try to read and speak with expression, because I really have no desire to bore anyone to tears!

Book

Johnston, Tony. 1983. *The Vanishing Pumpkin.* Illustrated by Tomie dePaola. New York: Putnam's Sons.

Summary: A 700-year-old woman and an 800-year-old man search for their pumpkin in order to make pumpkin pie. During their search, they meet a ghoul, a rapscallion, a varmint, and a wizard. Many tricks are played during the search, but the wizard pleasantly surprises them all in the end.

Prereading: Display the cover of the book. Discuss the title and cover illustrations. Have students predict what time of year the story takes place and which holiday is celebrated at this time. Predict where the pumpkin might have vanished to. Make guesses about whether the pumpkin was ever recovered after vanishing.

Unique Words or Concepts: ghoul, rapscallion, varmint, wizard, jack-o'-lantern

Questions for Discussion

1. Is this story reality or fantasy? What clues help you determine this?
2. When does the story take place?
3. Were the man and woman angry with the wizard for taking their pumpkin? Why or why not?
4. Have any of the students ever made/eaten pumpkin pie? Discuss where, when, what they thought of it.

Activities

1. Teach a mini-unit on pumpkins. Use journals to record responses to activities.

2. Visit a pumpkin patch as a class field trip.

3. Observe pumpkins. Describe how they feel, look, and smell. Compare

different types and sizes of pumpkins. Compare and contrast an orange and a pumpkin.

4. Measure pumpkins. Measure circumference. Make predictions about the weight of pumpkins based on observations and measurements. Are taller, wider, shorter, fatter pumpkins heavier? Use five different pumpkins. Put them in order from lightest to heaviest according to predictions. Weigh pumpkins and compare results to predictions.

5. Pumpkins and water. Chooses pumpkins of varying weights. Make predictions about whether they will float. Place pumpkins in water. Explain that the air space in the center makes it less dense, so it doesn't displace water. Predict if pieces of pumpkins will float. Test and discuss. Use other fruits and compare and contrast results.

6. Read It's Pumpkin Time! By Zoe Hall, From Seed to Jack-o'-Lantern by Hannah Lyons Johnson, or The Pumpkin Patch by Elizabeth King. Trace the growth of a pumpkin from a seed to a jack-o'-lantern.

7. Read poem October Fun. Discuss the fact that the object described is never actually named. Have students write a poem about an object without naming it.

8. Read poem Happy Jack-o-Lantern. Ask children to listen for what kind of jack-o'-lantern it is, how its face and eyes look, where it sits, and when it sits there. Discuss. Have students draw a picture to go with the poem. Make a class book.

9. Display two differently sized pumpkins in classroom. Have students place a counter or tally mark in front of the pumpkin that they think has the most seeds. After everyone has had a chance to make a guess, cut into the pumpkins and count the seeds.

10. Use the seeds from previous activity and bake them for students to taste.

11. Bake pumpkin pie for students to taste.

12. Use pumpkins from field trip and have a pumpkin/jack-o'-lantern decorating contest.

Companion Books

Benarde, Anita. 1972. The Pumpkin Smasher. New York: Walker.
Cavagnaro, David. 1979. Pumpkin People. San Francisco: Sierra Club Books.

Dillon, Jana. 1992. *Jeb Scarecrow's Pumpkin Patch*. Boston: Houghton Mifflin.

Friskey, Margaret. 1990. *The Perky Little Pumpkin: A Halloween Story*. Chicago: Children's Press.

Gendusa, Sam. 1989. *Carving Jack-o'-Lanterns*. Dayton, OR: SG Productions.

Greene, Ellin. 1970. *The Pumpkin Giant*. New York: Lothrop, Lee & Shepard.

Hall, Zoe. 1994. *It's Pumpkin Time!* New York: Scholastic.

Hellsing, Lennart. 1976. *The Wonderful Pumpkin*. New York: Atheneum.

Johnson, Hannah Lyons. 1974. *From Seed to Jack-o'-Lantern*. New York: Lothrop, Lee & Shepard.

Katz, Ruth J. 1979. *Pumpkin Personalities*. New York: Walker.

King, Elizabeth. 1990. *The Pumpkin Patch*. New York: Dutton.

Kroll, Steven. 1984. *The Biggest Pumpkin Ever*. New York: Holiday House.

Martin, Patricia Miles. 1966. *The Pumpkin Patch*. New York: Putnam.

McDonald, Megan. 1992. *The Great Pumpkin Switch*. New York: Orchard Books.

Rockwell, Anne. 1989. *Apples and Pumpkins*. New York: Macmillan.

Titherington, Jeanne. 1986. *Pumpkin, Pumpkin*. New York: Greenwillow Books.

Tudor, Tasha. 1962. *Pumpkin Moonshine*. New York: H. Z. Walck.

Yezback, Steven A. 1969. *Pumpkinseeds*. Indianapolis: Bobbs-Merrill. ❚

❚ This nontraditional student decided that instead of telling a story from a previously published children's book, she would tell a story that she herself wrote, based upon a family experience. She told the story effortlessly and was greeted with many complimentary comments from her peers. She told us that this story had really happened. From then on, whenever the roads were slick outside, you could invariably hear someone in class say, "Watch out, birds may be icky!"

Public speaking has been a lifelong struggle for me. I avoided it in any form for many years. I finally realized that there wasn't any way to completely avoid the necessity of being able to get up in front of a group of people. I took a special class for people with public speaking anxiety and I can now do a reasonable job of giving a speech.

I believe that being able to do public speaking is going to be vitally important to me as a teacher. I'll have many occasions when I will be speaking to parents, colleagues and children. I now seem to welcome opportunities to speak because the more practice I get, the better I get at speaking. I discovered that my anxiety about speaking decreased a great deal just by learning how to organize what I wanted to say. I was never taught how to prepare a speech but was required to give them!

I also believe that it's important to learn how to be a reasonably good storyteller. I like the feeling of not being tied to a book but being tied to the audience instead. I believe that storytelling is an effective way to get children interested in literature. Letting them participate in storytelling will also stimulate more reading of good literature.

My story for storytelling is a family story that I wrote. My son was intrigued by road signs when he was learning to read. Once on a long trip he read a sign to us that said "Birds may be icky." Later we found out it really said "Bridges may be icy."

I was happy to receive so many positive comments from my peers after telling this story! I really do want to work further on it and perhaps submit it for publication!

Birds May Be Icky

Story Problem

A little boy is learning to read and especially likes road signs. He misreads the sign Bridges May Be Icy. He thinks that it says Birds May Be Icky.

Sequence

1. Once there was a little boy who loved road signs. He would take his small wooden signs with him in the car and try to match them to the signs along the road.

2. When he was 2 years old his favorite signs were Stop and Yield. When his Grandma came to visit she would draw Stop and Yield over and over again on many sheets of paper. Before long the little boy could read Stop and Yield by himself.

3. As the little boy grows older he notices that signs are many different shapes and colors.

4. He sees signs that are circles like RR Crossing and Do Not Enter.

5. He sees signs shaped like rectangles and learns that these signs tell you what to do or what not to do.

6. His Mom reads the words on the signs to him but he knows that the sign with the big letter P and a red circle with a line across it means No Parking.

7. Sometimes his Mom reads the speed limit signs to his Dad in a very loud voice and this confuses the little boy because he knows that his Dad already knows how to read. He also is confused by the One Way signs that he sees.

8. Before long, the little boy turns five and learns some new signs when the

police officer teaches him and some other children how to walk to school safely. He learns Walk and Don't Walk and the School Crossing sign.

9. On his first day of school he sees a sign that is spelled O-U-T. That becomes his favorite sign later on because it means he and the other children get to go outside for recess.

10. Everyday at school the little boy learns new letters, new words and made lots of new friends. He soon can read the sign inside the door that says OUT on good weather days and IN on bad weather days.

11. Before long it was time for his long Spring Break from school. He and his family travel 425 miles to his grandparents' farm. He sees many different signs along the interstate highway.

12. He sees a diamond-shaped yellow sign and tries to read it. He frowns and says, "What a Useless Sign!" His family doesn't know what he means. He says, "That sign back there. It said, 'Birds May Be Icky!'"

13. His Dad sees the bridge in his rear view mirror and laughs. He says, "That sign says Bridges May Be Icy, not Birds May Be Icky!" The whole family laughs.

14. When he arrives at his grandparents' farm he tells them his funny story.

15. After dinner, he and his grandma draw "Bridges May Be Icy" on many sheets of paper except once in a while they draw "Birds May Be Icky" and laugh and laugh.

Conclusion

Learning to read can be fun. Everybody makes mistakes when reading but it doesn't matter and it may even be very funny.

Materials

Road signs and an OUT/IN sign. School supply stores have large packages of signs for about $7.00 and small packages for about $3.00.

Follow-Up Activities

1. Look at the yellow signs and discuss the differences between the words Bridges/Birds and Icy/Icky.

2. Discuss making mistakes when reading. Lead discussion toward the fact that mistakes are natural and may even be funny.

3. Show other environmental print signs and go for a walk inside and outside of school, looking for the signs in the story and other important signs like EXIT.

4. Have students arrange the signs in the same sequence that they appear in the story.

5. Discuss slang words using Icky as an example of words we all know and use but are not in the dictionary.

6. Discuss the colors and shapes of signs and what each one represents.

References

Crews, Donald. 1980. *Truck*. New York: Greenwillow Books.

Gibbons, Gail. 1993. *Puff-Flash-Bang! A Book About Signals*. New York: Morrow Junior Books.

Goor, Ron, and Nancy Goor. 1983. *Signs*. New York: Thomas Y. Crowell.

Helfman, Elizabeth S. 1967. *Signs & Symbols Around the World*. New York: Lothrop, Lee & Shepard.

Hoban, Tana. 1983. *I Read Signs*. New York: Greenwillow Books.

Hoban, Tana. 1983. *I Read Symbols*. New York: Greenwillow Books.

Lubell, Winifred. 1972. *Picture Signs & Symbols*. New York: Parent's Magazine Press. ▮

▮ This reflection and artifact are the work of a nontraditional student in a secondary language arts methods course. She decided, after raising her children and pursuing a successful career in business, that she had a passion to teach. Through this artifact she reflects and illustrates how important her recognition of the fear she had once had about speaking in front of groups was to her understanding her students' apprehension. Furthermore, this student showed how necessary it is for all of us to do what we ask our students to do.

I included this first draft of a poem in progress that I am writing about speaking. I am a speaker, but that has not always been the case. I know, though, that my students must be speakers, and I must model my own strategies for them. I am the more capable peer. I must show my students not only how difficult it is to speak in front of others, but also how I have made it easier.

I also believe that in student talk I can find out a plethora of information that I need to be a better teacher. I must take special care, however, to be accepting of what I hear, when they speak.

I Am a Speaker . . .

I remember a time,
when having to speak
to other than family or friends,
was the most painful,
most awful,
most dreaded of events.
At the thought of having to speak,
to ask or answer a question,
I would blush
and feel flushed,
and at times become quite nauseous.
But all of that was so long ago,
that I'm not sure when it changed.
For now I no longer dread speaking.
It is because of my experiences
that I decided that Speech
was what I would like to teach.
And so I began my course of study
of speech of which there were many.
And over the semesters I have learned much
about the role of speech in groups,
interpersonal relationships,
persuasion and organizations.
But it was this semester that I learned,
that there is more to being a speaker,
than introductions, and organization, and conclusions.
It was while reading for my course in Speech Methods,
that I began to understand
the importance of speech in learning,
or student talk, as it was fondly called.
In one of those books the author stated that,
much more than all of the papers they write,
or the worksheets, or even the tests,

it is student talk that really shows,
the learning that is taking place,
in the classroom and even the hall.
So now when I say that I am a speaker,
it reflects more than just my ability.
It also shows my belief that unless I encourage my students to speak,
I'll never really understand the learning that is taking place. ❙

8 | I Am a Teacher and a Learner

Teaching, like any art, is an endless cycle of trial and error. Keep thinking, keep reading and discussing, and changing and experimenting.   Mem Fox

Teaching is hardly a static profession. As teachers learn and grow as professionals, so too do their classrooms. Teachers must consider themselves learners as well, modeling for students the processes of reading, writing, and learning.

The artifacts in this section reflect this notion of the teacher as a learner. Teachers write about their teaching philosophies, which change as they attend conferences, read, observe other teachers, and talk about teaching with others. Questioning our beliefs about teaching and learning makes us more reflective and, in turn, more effective teachers. Teachers also include sample lessons and units they have written that encourage students to be actively involved with their own learning.

A third-grade teacher that we know said, "Once I get comfortable in my teaching, I know it's time to change." Encouraging teachers to examine their own teaching and learning is one way to keep all of us from getting too comfortable in our own teaching.

▍ This first-year special education teacher connects the roots to becoming a teacher to his teaching philosophy. He never planned to be a teacher, but things seemed to turn out that way. His work in special education and his insights into working with this special group of young people are also highlighted.

Teacher and learner *are two words that really go together. In order to be a teacher you have to be a learner first. In order to be successful in life you must continue to learn every day.*

I thought about why I became a teacher. This personal insight was something about myself that I never sat down and wrote about. It taught me the importance of being a teacher and a learner too.

Why Did I Choose to Become a Teacher?

I never thought I would be a teacher, much less a special education teacher. It really never crossed my mind when I was little that I was going to be a teacher.

I dreamed like all little boys of being a big league baseball player. In fact, I did not even think I was going to go to college. When I did go to college it was tough to decide on a major. First, I was going to be a newspaper columnist, then I was going to do something in the communication field, then I was going to be a historical researcher, and finally I was going to be a history and journalism high school teacher that coached basketball and baseball. Funny, it seems that you never exactly turn out the way you want to be, because now I think I am going to be a special education teacher.

A special education teacher? How did this all come about? I think sometimes in life things happen for a reason. About four years ago I was just living a life where I really did not have many goals. I was living paycheck to paycheck and really did not know what I wanted to do for the rest of my life. One of my friends asked me to volunteer for this bowling league on Sundays. He said I would be working with adults that have disabilities. I was scared because I really did not know how to react. What I found was people that still influence me today. These adults, along with the many students that I have worked with, have made me a better person today than I was four years ago. They have given me "gifts" such as hope, patience, and the respect for the little things in life. For all of these things I am deeply grateful. So grateful that the only thing left for me to do was to find a way to help them out to the best of my ability and I feel teaching is the answer. One person told me once that once you volunteer to help out with the "special people" you never walk away from them. Well, I have not walked away from them in four years and do not plan on doing it anytime soon.

My teaching philosophy has changed about as much as my majors in college. I started out with those great expectations that many teachers start out with when they begin teaching that I was going to be different and change all these students' lives. I was going to be the teacher that turned all the bad students around. Using the traditional education curriculum combined with my enthusiasm, I knew I was in a can't lose situation. I was going to be successful and this would be a very easy job.

Well, reality set in real quick when I student taught for the first time. I realized this was not going to be an easy job and I really better sit down and figure out what my teaching philosophy is.

I see myself adding to and taking away from my philosophy. I do not think a teacher can have a very strict never any exceptions type of philosophy. The students we have today are all different kinds of learners so I do not think this approach would work with all learners. On the other hand I believe that limits must be set for all students. The basis of my philosophy is that any student that enters my social studies, journalism, or special education classroom leave with a sense of self. That they know a little bit more about themselves and where they are going. The students I hope will be a little bit more open-minded than they were when they first took my class. My goal as their teacher is to reach the highest potential they can achieve or do the best they can with what they have. This is the basis of my philosophy, however, I have to be flexible. I realize each student is different and that to some students I might be a father figure, an adult, a friend, or a counselor. Even though this gets away from the traditional teacher role I realize some students need that part of me too.

I feel we all are teachers and students in this world. Sometimes we forget that our students teach us more than we can ever teach them. After all I think it was Socrates that said we all learn by contrast. Knowing that as a teacher I am not afraid to try new things and new materials if it helps a student with a different learning style learn something that he or she could never learn before.

I did not choose to be a teacher, but many people say I make a good one. I do not know if this is something I will do for the rest of my life but right now I enjoy getting up in the morning and going to school. When that enjoyment is gone it will be time to get out, but right now I do not see that happening. ▌

▌ This is Kathy's teaching philosophy. I wrote this originally when I was nominated for a teaching award. I have revised and refined it every year, as my views about teaching and learning change. I am a teacher who does what she asks her students to do. I model reading, writing, listening, and speaking with my students. I also learn a great deal from my students.

I am a teacher and a learner together. One cannot stand without the other, in my opinion. I will never know everything as a teacher, but I can strive to do better and to learn from and with my students.

My teaching philosophy was easy to write. I think the main part of teaching for me is creating a community of learners. Often I do this with food, because when you eat with others you are more likely to talk to them and listen to them. Food also allows for a comfort level in learning and really helps to establish a community of learners. Talking and listening are important components of how I set up my classes because they are the ways in which I learn from others.

When I returned home from my first day of school as a kindergartener, I knew that I would be a teacher one day. I loved school then and I still do today. I cannot imagine another job that is more challenging, rewarding, and diverse. I have taught elementary, secondary, undergraduate, and graduate students. I love the process of teaching. I think a teacher should be an enthusiastic model of lifelong learning. A good teacher is passionate about the subject area and a facilitator of learning. I try to establish in my own classes a community of readers and writers. I am a member of this community, but I am not the only teacher in it. I learn from my students because I listen to them and I value their input. I try to motivate students to take responsibility for their own learning by modeling my own learning process with them. I read to my students from fine literature and I share my writing with them. In turn, I listen to them read their own writing and from good books. I give demonstrations, teach lessons, and then invite my students to do the same. We learn from each other, as well as from related research and other resources.

I also think students deserve teachers who know who they are. I take pride in the fact that I know all of my students' names every semester and that I know something about each student. This is a challenge, especially since I have nearly 65 students a semester, but it is extremely important to them and to me. During my time as an undergraduate and graduate student, I can only remember a handful of professors who actually knew my name. The ones that did were the best teachers I had because they took the time to get to know me and what I wanted and needed to learn. This personal touch had a great impact on me and shaped my own philosophy of teaching.

The following quote by eighth-grade teacher and author Linda Rief, reflects my own philosophy of teaching:

> What do I want for my students? I want them to leave my classroom knowing they are readers and writers, wanting to learn more, and having a number of strategies for that learning in any field. I want them to like learning and to like themselves. I want them to know they have important things to say and unique ways of saying them. I want them to know their voices are valued. I want learning to be fun. Most importantly, I want them to gain independence as learners, knowing and trusting their own choices. (Rief 1992, 4)

I think the best teachers are learners themselves, constantly examining their beliefs and practices, modeling the lifelong process of learning.

Rief, L. 1992. *Seeking diversity: Language arts with adolescents.* Portsmouth, NH: Heinemann. ❚

❚ This undergraduate student attended our state reading conference and wrote about what she learned from this experience. She talks about the importance of lifelong learning and professional growth throughout one's teaching career.

Attending the State Reading Conference in Kearney was an important step in my education. It showed me that teachers never stop learning and that teachers learn from each other all the time.

I wrote about several sessions I attended in the following artifact. They got me excited about teaching by talking about all the neat things they do in their classes and the types of reading and writing that their students do.

I now realize that professional development is an important part of teaching too. I can't just assume that after I graduate with my teaching degree that I'll know all the answers. I'll always be searching for a better way to teach something and that's okay. In fact, that's probably good because it means that I'll still be learning. Maybe knowing all the answers isn't the main part of being a teacher. Maybe having questions about how to get better is more important.

My trip to Kearney, Nebraska, was a wonderful learning experience. The atmosphere at the conference was friendly, the speakers were great, and the workshops were the best. I came home feeling like I had really obtained practical and useful information.

My favorite part of the conference was the workshops. Here are three (besides yours) that I'd like to remember. The first one was entitled "Taking Care of Business." Two wonderful first-grade teachers from the Millard school district discussed managing a reading and writing classroom. The best thing about this workshop was the fact that these teachers shared all kinds of great ideas for organizing a classroom. A few of these great tips were: keeping a box on their desk that said notes for the teacher. Then when kids would bring in notes in the morning they wouldn't all be bombarding the teacher at the same time while she's trying to get organized. Also having weekly responsibilities was a good idea. Each child would fill out a check list with the responsibilities they would accomplish that week. That would really help the first graders learn responsibilitiy. They had a great attendance chart on which the children would automatically come in and pull a slip to show they were present and also put a hot or cold lunch slip on the chart. These were teacher-tested because they were the things that these two women do in their classrooms every day. They also shared all kinds of tips from using a timer at the computer to how to create poetry books. Of the their best ideas involved taking snapshots of their students. They used these photos throughout the year, in the sub folder, for graphing activities, and working with reading on sentence strips. They also showed a cute slide show that they had used with their students' parents on curriculum night. We were able to actually see their classrooms and how they were set up. They also gave us a super packet with some of their ideas in it. This was a perfect seminar for someone like me, who has not set up a classroom yet!

My next workshop was entitled "Buddies, Books, and Bright Ideas." This was one of my favorites! I received a huge packet of ideas on using buddies in your classroom. The presenters were two wonderful fourth-grade teachers from Millard. They shared so many ideas! First they explained all about buddies and how to get started. They they gave us all kinds of wonderful examples of the many activities their fourth graders did with the first graders in their building. Buddies work well between an older grade and a younger grade. Some ideas included: writing letters, partner reading, different art activities, and many holiday ideas. My favorite holiday activity was having the fourth-grade students sneak into the classroom when the first graders are gone and to leave green candy and gold dust and little green leprechaun footprints on the desk. There were also many ideas that involved real learning objectives. I have seen lots of buddy programs at work and I think they are super. This workshop gave me tons of ideas to use when I have my own buddy program.

My final workshop for the weekend was "Literature in the Reading-Writing Classroom." This was a pretty good presentation. The teacher, from Peru, was the most energetic woman I've ever seen. She was a crazy lady! She had so much to share that she didn't get halfway through. But she did give us a great packet and shared some wonderful ideas. She had kinds of big books with her and she showed us the many different books her first graders had written. My favorite was the book about shoes that her class made. They took pictures of different shoes all around the school. Then they made a big book and wrote about the many types of shoes in their school. Another helpful idea she gave in her packet was activities involving a variety of Cinderella stories. I think it is really neat for students to learn about fairy tales from different cultures. I was really happy with her presentation and her handouts, I think they could be really helpful.

The Nebraska State Reading Conference was the best experience for me. Listening to real teachers is the most useful and practial thing I can do to help myself prepare to teach. It was a wonderful experience and I am so glad I went. ∎

∎ This first-year teacher created a web or integrated unit on prairie life and Nebraska (a topic covered in her fourth-grade classroom). She collected many ideas and books to enhance her curriculum regarding this required subject.

The following artifact is my web on Prairie Life/Nebraska History. I have tried to make this unit as interesting and fun as possible. I plan on using it next semester when we learn about Nebraska history. I enjoyed writing it and am anxious to do many of the activities. I think they will teach my students a great deal more about Nebraska than they would learn from just reading about it in a textbook.

Gathering children's books on the topic was great fun. I am always amazed at what wonderful children's books there are on so many diverse topics! I think the books and activities I have selected will help my students make connections about prairie life and the history of our state in a way that an expository piece from a textbook could not.

I am proud of my web. It shows that I can create meaningful activities for my students because I know my students. It gives me the confidence I need to encourage more meaningful connections for my students, rather than just relying on a textbook.

Homes

Books

Bunting, E. 1995. *Dandelions*. San Diego: Harcourt Brace.
Lawlor, L. 1986. *Addie across the prairie*. Niles, IL: Whitman.
Lawlor, L. 1989. *Addie's Dakota winter*. Niles, IL: Whitman.
Miller, Mary Britton. 1988. "Houses." In *Sing a song of popcorn*, by B. S.
    deRegniers. New York: Scholastic.
Rounds, G. 1995. *Sod houses on the great plains*. New York: Holiday House.

Activities

1. List the advantages and disadvantages of sod houses and homes now. Compare and contrast sod houses and now.

2. Make a scale model of a sod house. Use mud cakes or pieces of sod to make the house. Plant grass seeds or dandelions on the roof.

3. Measure off an area in the classroom of the dimensions of a typical sod house. They were usually twelve feet by fourteen feet or sixteen feet by twenty feet. Have groups of four or five students be a family unit and "live" in the marked off area. What would be some problems living in such cramped quarters?

4. In the book *Sod Houses on the Great Plains*, homesteaders put grease on a piece of paper to let light in. Make your own window by rubbing Crisco on a piece of paper. How long does the window stay? What can you see out of it? Use them for windows in the sod houses as described in number two above.

5. How would you feel if you were Mama in the book *Dandelions*? Pretend you are Mama and write several journal entries chronicling her feelings from the moment she came to Nebraska to a few months after settling in. Do her feelings change?

6. Read *Addie Across the Prairie* and *Addie's Dakota Winter*. Discuss the hardships Addie's family faced. Why was the house so important to early homesteaders? How did the house affect the family?

7. Read the poem "Houses" out loud and discuss how homes have dramatically changed through the years. Is the description of early homes in the poem accurate?

Famous People

Books

Carpenter, A. 1978. *The new enchantment of America: Nebraska*. Chicago: Children's Press.

Conrad, P. 1991. *Praire visions: The life and times of Solomon Butcher*. New York: HarperCollins.

Hargrove, J. 1989. *America the beautiful: Nebraska*. Chicago: Children's Press.

Ringgold, F. 1993. *Dinner at Aunt Connie's house*. New York: Hyperion.

Sharp, N. L. 1993. *Today I'm going fishing with my dad*. Honesdale, PA: Boyds Mills Press.

Activities

1. Choose a famous Nebraskan and write an acrostic poem using their last name. Use words which describe the person.

2. Read *Dinner at Aunt Connie's House*. Using the same format, choose seven famous Nebraskans to "talk" to the reader. Include their picture and important information about their life.

3. Make a list of famous Nebraskans. Survey parents, older siblings, and relatives to see if they know what each person is famous for. Make a class graph of the results. Prepare "study sheets" on those people that were not well know and give them to the parents, etc.

4. Watch a movie a famous Nebraskan is in or read a book written by a Nebraskan. Respond in some manner. Movies: Fred Astaire, Henry Fonda, Marlon Brando. Books: Willa Cather, Mari Sandoz, John Neihardt, N. L. Sharp.

5. On a Nebraska map, place one end of a length of string on the town where a famous Nebraskan was born. Secure the other end away from the map. Put the person's picture and a brief description of the person next to the string.

6. Read the book *Prairie Visions*. Write a story or journal entry about one of the pictures in the book.

Schools

Books

Houston, G. 1992. *My Great-Aunt Arizona*. New York: HarperCollins.

Kalman, B. 1982. *Early schools*. New York: Crabtree.

Kalman, B. 1994. *A one-room school*. New York: Crabtree.

Activities

1. Using the glossary from Bobbie Kalman's books, make an ABC book of school terms that are seldom used now (such as: stave, blotting paper, etc.).

2. Re-create a one-room school house in the classroom. Pretend to put fire in the stove, use slates, have a dunce corner, recite facts and poems. Debrief at the end of the day. What did they like? Not like?

3. Play Fox and Goose or Ante Ante Over the Shanty at recess. These games are described in *Early Schools*.

4. Obey the rules for teachers and students on pages 42–43 in the book *Early Schools*. Compare and contrast school rules now and in early schools. Are there any rules that are still the same or similar?

5. Discuss or write your answer to the following question: In your opinion, have schools improved over the years? Why or why not?

6. Make a T-chart with "old-fashioned" school terms and terms that we use today that are comparable.

Quilts

Books

Bolton, J. 1993. *My grandmother's patchwork quilt*. New York: Doubleday.
Meigs, L. 1993. *Nebraska from A to Z*. Omaha: Linda Meigs Studio.
Polacco, P. 1988. *The keeping quilt*. New York: Simon & Schuster.

Activities

1. Do some research on the history of quilt patterns. Make up your own quilt pattern and name it. What considerations did you have in naming the quilt? Put each classmates piece together to make a classroom quilt.

2. Read *The Keeping Quilt*. Ask Mom, Dad, or another relative if there is a special quilt in the family. Who made it? What were the squares made of? Bring the quilt or take a picture of it and present it to the class.

3. Many quilts represent a story or a series of events. If the class were to make a quilt chronicling events during the school year, what would be

included? Make a list of milestones during the school year and create a class quilt.

4. Choose one page in the book N*ebraska from* A *to* Z. Take notes from that page and list them on an index card. Make the quilt square from that page using geometric pieces of paper and paste the index card in the middle of it. Put everyone's squares together to form a large quilt about Nebraska.

5. Using the book N*ebraska from* A *to* Z as a starting point, predict why quilt patterns were given their names. Does the name fit the pattern? Should the pattern be called something else?

6. Read the book M*y Grandmother's Patchwork* Quilt and make the quilt pieces provided.

7. Using the quilt in M*y Grandmother's Patchwork* Quilt, write a story about the quilt pieces.

Feelings/Images

Books

Bouchard, D. 1995. *If you're not from the prairie*. New York: Simon & Schuster.
Siebert, D. 1989. *Heartland*. New York: Crowell.
Wills, C. A. 1994. A *historical album of Nebraska*. Brookfield, CT: Millbrook
    Press.

Activities

1. Have someone read the books H*eartland* and I*f* You're N*ot from the* P*rairie* aloud. Have the rest of the class close their eyes and form images in thier minds. Discuss what images everyone formed. Show the pictures to the books.

2. Paint a mural of the images and feelings in the books listed above.

3. Write a poem which captures the feelings and images of early Nebraska. Write another poem which captures the feelings and images of Nebraska today. Discuss the differences between the poems.

4. Using the book I*f* You're N*ot from the* P*rairie* as a model, write a book about the city instead of the prairie. The whole class could write the story and groups of students could illustrate it.

Additional Books About the Prairie

Ernst, L. C. 1995. *Little Red Riding Hood: A newfangled prairie tale*. New York: Simon & Schuster.

Harvey, B. 1986. *My prairie year: Based on the diary of Elenore Plaisted*. New York: Holiday House.

Harvey, B. 1990. *My prairie Christmas*. New York: Holiday House.

MacLachlan, P. 1985. *Sarah, plain and tall*. New York: Harper.

MacLachlan, P. 1994. *Skylark*. New York: HarperCollins.

Van Leeuwen, J. 1992. *Going west*. New York: Dial.

Walker, B. M. 1979. *The Little House cookbook*. New York: Harper. ▌

▌ This artifact was one that was required in Sheri's secondary English/language arts course. Each student was asked to articulate his or her personal teaching philosophy. As the teacher of record in the course, Sheri also wrote and shared her own teaching philosophy. The following reflection and artifact are the work of a nontraditional student teacher in a local, and famous, school and home for "wayward" boys. Her philosophy was obviously affected by this experience, as became evident in the reading of these two pieces of her writing.

I included my teaching philosophy in my portfolio because it was required of me, and now, finally, I'm glad it was. I was forced to actually think about what I believe about my teaching, what I believe about learning. Much of what I believe about education has come from literature, and much from my life experiences. I've noted what works for me, what didn't work, and what is a waste of my, and my students', time.

My teaching philosophy, and the articulation of such, enables me to constantly ask the question: does this make sense? If the answer is "no," then I need to redirect. If the answer is "yes," then I know that the choices my students and I are making are valuable and will lead to them being able to make those excellent choices without me. I want my students to leave my classroom knowing they can do anything.

My Educational Philosophy

I once believed that teaching English involved reading beautiful literature and, in turn, learning to write with magnificant style. I've since concluded, however, that my passion can't and shouldn't be forced on others. It is mine and not theirs, afterall. Instead, I've decided that teaching English or any-thing else is about awakening and nurturing aspiration. Personal aspiration is key to a successful transistion from school to adult life.

As a teacher, it is my goal to help students learn the process of choice. It is my aspiration to aid each student in daring to become the best he/she can possibly become. This process involves risk, and my classroom will and must offer the youngsters I guide a supportive and safe environment.

Life centers on choice; I became certain of this after reading Steinbeck's *East of Eden* and mulling over Lee's translation of the Hebrew word "timshel." Lee decided that timshel is not an order, that it doesn't mean "Thou shalt," but, instead, that it puts resonsibility for choices made, squarely in the lap of the choice maker. Timshel means "Thou mayest." We, therefore, choose our individual paths and I, as educator, feel responsibility for creating an environment where students make individual choices.

My students will experience the anguish and triumph of exercising free will through the process of making individual decisions within thematic units which have been developed by me, the teacher. They will choose which writing assignment, which novel, which poems and short stories they wish to explore and complete. They may also propose new assignments not contained in my thematic units as alternative projects.

Fear of risk often involves fear of failure. If we fear risk and possible failure, we often fail to dare success. I, as a teacher, feel a need to create a supportive class environment where each is free to strive and attain, strive and fail, and strive again. Through our example, students learn to support others' efforts. I believe it is important for us to share personal triumphs and failures in order to enable students to realize mistakes as part of growth. Only after students realize it's OK to make a mistake, can the concepts of peer editing and critique be introduced. Peer editing and critique are critical components of the learning process because students learn to value the opinions of equals.

I aspire to guide students to personal bests, and I am therefore concerned with literacy. Literate people don't necessarily develop an abiding passion for Shakespeare or win Nobel prizes for literature. Literate people do read and write. They have an appreciation for the printed word and the ability to translate thoughts to paper. It is my job to find the keys that make reading a pleasure and writing a process. ∎

9 | I Am Self-Reflective

Evaluation in my classroom . . . must begin with a careful assessment of my own literate engagement. I cannot expect of children what I do not practice myself. Donald Graves

In our literacy classes, we both keep portfolios. We agree with Donald Graves. We cannot ask our students to do something we do not do ourselves. Thus we model the process of self-assessment. Our students have very little experience with self-evaluation and assessment. We find ourselves discussing strengths and weaknesses of our own learning to serve as models for our students in self-assessment.

Since self-assessment is so new and unfamiliar to our students, this section of our students' portfolios is often thin. We provide students with a self-evaluation sheet (see pp. 134–35) which forces them to take a good look at themselves as learners. Additionally, we use this self-evaluation sheet for our own assessment purposes as we keep anecdotal records on students throughout the semester. For instance, we note when a student shares a piece of writing in author's chair or when a student makes a particularly helpful suggestion to another writer. We also note when a student has taken a risk either in her writing, her reading, or her sharing of a compliment with a fellow community member. We celebrate daily these benchmarks of growth, sometimes with greeting cards, sometimes with notes, and sometimes with just a "I noticed that . . ." comment.

Giving students a voice in their own learning process is often a foreign concept to our students. Allowing their own students to self-assess is often new to them as well. For this reason the other artifacts in this section are class pulses that give our students a voice in the daily workings of our classes. Just as we invite our students to tell us how things are going, we ask that they will in turn give their students a similar voice in their own classrooms.

Most of the artifacts in this section do not have reflection pieces, because the self-assessment is reflective by its very nature.

❚ This is the self-evaluation sheet Sheri provided for her students in all of her courses using portfolio assessment. Many of the students are unfamiliar with the entire process of self-reflection and thinking about their own learning, and as a result they need more guidance than "Do a self-evaluation!" Many of the students wander from these questions, and I encourage that. This list, I explain, is only a place to start, if they are unsure of the direction a self-evaluation might take.

In addition, I follow up this reflection in the final portfolio conference. I tell the students I will be ending our discussion with what I consider the most important question: What next? What are your future literacy goals? I always mention that a portfolio is never finished, and that merely because our course together is over, that doesn't mean they are done with their portfolio. So, with that in mind, what happens next? The questions in this "nudge" are intended to guide students in that direction.

Self-Evaluation

Address your learning for this session. Discuss how you grew this session; how your attendance influenced this growth; how your reading/writing are evidence of growth; how your thinking might have changed or been supported by our discussions. Discuss your reading and its impact on your learning; how your portfolio represents this discussion, etc.

Possible self-evaluation questions

What's your greatest strength as a learner?

What are three of the most important things you are able to do as a reader?

In what ways have you grown as a reader this session? How did that happen? What would you like to be able to do better as a reader?

In what ways have you grown as a speaker this session? How did that happen? What would you like to be able to do better as a speaker?

In what ways have you grown as a writer this session? How did that happen? What would you like to be able to do better as a writer?

What grade would you give yourself in the following categories?

Writing	_____	Listening	_____
Reading	_____	Attitude	_____
Speaking	_____	Effort	_____

❙ This self-reflection was written by a nontraditional student in a secondary language arts methods course. She was concerned at the beginning of the course that she wouldn't be a good teacher because she didn't like to lecture. She wrote me a letter early in the semester voicing just that thought, and I responded that I certainly didn't see that as a reason to be worried. This delightful woman, full of energy, enthusiasm, and a passion for learning, and a wonderful coach for many years of her son's soccer teams, worried about this traditional model of what à teacher does.

Semester Self-Reflection

A lot of what I've learned this semester reinforces what I have always believed as a parent. Firstly, that young people are special and that we as adults need to value them for their individual qualities. We need to recognize the positive things young people have to offer and encourage them to continue to do their best. Their accomplishments should always be recognized—even the small ones—as well as their attempts. Young people need to feel safe—in a secure environment with someone they can trust and who they know trusts them. They must be allowed to make some mistakes, to stumble without dire consequences and then to know there is someone there to catch them before they fall. Young people need some autonomy. They need to have choices and their choices need to be respected.

I also learned this semester how important and valuable it is to write with my students. I try to model what I consider is positive behavior in other aspects of my life, so writing with my students only makes sense. I've learned that I don't have to lecture to be a good teacher, that I can do what makes sense for me and more importantly what makes sense for my students. I've learned that evaluations do not have to be all about grades (thank God). The value is in what our students learn on their own, not what we as teachers try to force into their heads.

I've learned to recognize the VALUE in evaluation and to teach 1/3 curriculum, 1/3 what students need to know, and 1/3 what I am passionate about.

I've seen firsthand that the best possible teacher is the one who lives what she teaches, and I thank you for that Sheri. ∎

∎ This self-reflection was written for an undergraduate content reading course. The preservice teacher who wrote the piece is a history/language arts major. Her writing illustrates how difficult this process was for her, but it also depicts how meaningful the process was as well.

Self-Evaluation

Thinking of myself as a learner has been a change of pace for an education class. It seems I am usually geared to be thinking of our students as learners, and not of myself at all. Through this new light I have been reminded of the importance of learning with students, and of setting a visible example of a successful learner for the students. It is probably true that students glean more from what the teacher is not teaching than from what the teacher thinks he/she is teaching. With this in mind, I have tried to take this opportunity to look objectively at myself as a learner, and to synthesize the reasons for my success as a student, and as a reader in particular.

Somehow, I had lost sight of the relationship between my learning and that of my students-to-be, prior to this class. Further, I had neglected my reading and had become so caught up in the have-to-read of text books, that thinking about teaching reading to students in all classes presented itself as a new revelation. I have taken time to look at my reading habits, and my reading pleasures, and this has helped me to see new ways that I can help students succeed in school. Too often I have looked at teaching as having the ability to explain things well. This seems more the job of a tutor than a teacher now. I had not realized how my reading skills have helped me through many subjects, and I hope I can teach some of these skills to students to make learning more fun and less work.

Through the years of school I have relied heavily on my ability to write. I am not speaking of my ability to write stories or poems, nor am I referring to a phenomenal vocabulary. I have been told that I write well, I suppose this just means I can transpose thoughts relatively clearly, well enough to be understood. Whenever I have had essay exams, my ability to write logically and concisely has pulled me through, especially when I have not felt sure of the material. When I think of the students who lack confidence in their writing, or lack writing skills, I realize how much harder they have to work, and how much more pressure they must be putting on themselves. Although I feel I have talent for writing, I also believe it to be limited. I love to read, what a great gift these authors get to share with others. I hope to improve my creative writing skills. I have worked on illustrations for a children's book and would love to write them. This class has given me some hope, I really want to take some writing classes.

Both of these components, reading and writing, are critical thinking skills crucial for scholastic success. I realize now that these skills cannot be taught in language arts classes along, they must be taught in every class. This is very important at the senior high level, as classes begin to specialize, and with each specialty comes a unique set of reading and writing skills, that when understood and used, make the learning process more fluent. We offer technical writing classes at the college level, but we do not teach our high school students how to write in different ways, if at all. I believe that I have learned a great deal about what my responsibilities as a teacher are, from this class.

My growth as a reader this session has taken shape in my trying to accept less stringent standards for myself. I was surprised to hear so few other students comment on their obsession with reading every word. I am compulsive about it, not only do I read every word, if it is new to me I rehearse pronouncing it until I can do so with ease (especially in science). This compulsion has slowed my reading down, and this has frustrated me. Somehow, hearing that "speed reading" is not cheating, that it is, in fact, a strategy of successful readers, has made it easier for me to consider. I guess in some sense, I have learned to skip or skim material when necessary, but I am trying to improve my reading speed. I think I will probably be able to do more reading for pleasure if I can do this.

I had not thought about teaching students how to read science, only how to understand it. I see clearly now, that this deprives them of the opportunity to teach themselves in their own style. There are numerous tricks that years of school have taught me about reading for art, and in particular, science classes. I never thought of teaching students these "tricks." I wonder what my high school and college experience would have been like if someone had taught me some of the tricks, how much precious time could've been saved. I guess that we assume students know these things, once they become second nature to us we forget that not everyone else experiences the same things. My reading skills have improved since the birth of my son. Time is so much more limited now, I have had to pare down what I have to do, what I can do, and what I'd like to do if I have the time. These organizational skills could be useful for any student.

Speaking and listening skills are also important for school success. This class has caused me to reflect on what those skills are, and how I have interpreted them for my own level of success. I am not someone who really minds speaking in front of other people, but my short tether for annoyance keeps me from doing so very often. Instead, I listen, and I try to listen attentively to everything around me. As a child I was a stickler for exact words, I could repeat anything exactly, and expected exact applications. I have since tried to let up, without lessening my attention.

My growth in these areas, I suppose, must lie in my newfound appreciation for discussion skills, and the need to teach them, as we do not seem to come by them naturally, and as many students are shown very poor examples at home. In our small group discussions other students often commented on the poor listening and discussing skills they observe in their college classes. In the text, Mrs. K. explained how she took her students through the discussion process, step-by-step, and let the students explain to her why these "rules of conversation" are useful and important. She listened to them, thus modeling what she wanted them to learn. From time to time I think that I should force myself to speak more in class. I guess I too, am a victim of poor listening/speaking skills. When I feel that others do not value what I have to say, I refrain from speaking, and when I sense that others are looking to argue with different points of view, I hold my tongue. I hope that I can learn to discuss more comfortably with my students, and that I can instill in them the importance of respecting the opinions of others.

I feel uncomfortable grading myself, this is something new for me. I would love to do this with my students. It seems funny that when we receive grades most say they earned an "A," but that teacher gave me an "F." I guess this system would alleviate this problem, again, giving students claim to their education and what they get out of it. This really shows me that teaching is not active and learning passive, students cannot expect to be taught and invest nothing.

So, I will give myself grades . . . Writing A, I haven't written this much in quite some time . . . Reading A, I have read voraciously this session and will continue to do so . . . Speaking B, I don't speak much in front of large groups, but I have been a willing contributor in small groups, I hope I have offered something of interest to the other group members, at least when I speak I try to watch their cues and speak in accordance . . . Listening A, if I do nothing else well, I really do listen to others, and I have learned a lot from listening in this class, we've had a lot to listen to . . . Attitude A, I hope that I enter every class with a desire to learn and to grow, I think of each class as an opportunity, I hope it shows . . . Effort A, this is so difficult to gauge, it is one of those areas that has been drilled into my head as measurable only by comparison to others in the class. But I feel that I have tried, I always make an effort to be in class, to be on time, to listen and to show appreciation, I have also tried to put my personal growth on the line and look at myself in a new way. I feel this class has been a good example of what education should be like . . . if it is what one makes of it, I have really enjoyed this class and have learned a lot. **∎**

∎ This author was a nontraditional undergraduate student with five children of her own. She would often linger after class to visit with Kathy or to ask questions. She shared her own reading and writing frequently with the class and really listened to and learned from her classmates. The following piece was at the beginning of her portfolio to illustrate what she had learned throughout the semester. I was pleased to see the last line especially, since creating a community of learners is my goal as a professor. I felt that this student understood what we had been doing in class by sharing our own reading and writing with one another.

I Have Learned

I have learned that knowing how to spell or the fine points of grammar and punctuation do not a good writer make. Good writing comes with practice. Good writing comes with sharing part of yourself with the reader.

I have learned that a child needs to be read to and to read to become a reader.

I have learned that we need to model listening, speaking, writing and reading to children, so that they will know that it is worthwhile.

I have learned that we are only the guides. We give children the tools that help them discover the world.

I have learned to approach teaching in a holistic child-centered way.

I have learned that children learn to read, write, and spell in much the same way as they learn to walk and talk. And all efforts on their part are to be encouraged.

I have learned how important it is to give children time in class to read and write whatever they wish.

I have learned that one can learn more when one shares (one's writings, thoughts, books, feelings).

I have learned that children can help each other.

I have learned that I can integrate any subject with any other subject.

I have learned to make connections.

I have learned that "It's a damn poor mind that can think of only one way to spell a word." Andrew Jackson.

I have learned that if I want children to be effective communicators, I need to communicate effectively.

I have learned how to build a community of learners. ▌

▌ This teacher was taking the last class in her master's program. She had learned a great deal about integration and had included many examples from her own students in her portfolio. She thought a lot about how she might improve what she was doing in her classroom. Probably the most significant thing this student did was to share her personal writing. She has written a manuscript of a children's book based upon a family story. She shared this with the class and has worked on publishing it. This model of a writer is a powerful one for her students. She practices what she teaches and her students respect her. Her students also see the value in writing because of the modeling of their teacher.

Self-Assessment

My growth as a graduate student, elementary teacher, reader and writer can best be measured through the items in my portfolio. I have carefully selected items which I think demonstrate my growth in and dedication to literacy. The following items are presented in this portfolio:

1. *Teaching Philosophy*: My philosophy regarding the teaching of language arts has been influenced by experts such as Mem Fox, Donald Graves, Bernice Cullinan, Glenna Davis Sloan, and Ken Goodman. My beliefs are passionately expressed in my philosophy statement. It is important for me to be able to confidently express my teaching philosophy to my students, their parents, and my colleagues. Knowing the research behind many of the ideas I believe in helps me articulate my philosophy.

2. *Book Sharing of Brown Angles: An Album of Pictures and Verse*: I fell in love with the poetry complemented by the antique photographs in this book. It is a beautiful book to use in developing cultural pride. In addition to my lesson, I have included some baby picture poetry that my students wrote after I read *Brown Angels* to them.

3. *Response Log and Literature Guide to The Giver by Lois Lowry*: *The Giver* is a haunting story that stayed with me long after I finished reading it. Lowry has created a world without crime, disease, disrespect, or memories of unpleasant events. At first, this world appears to be appealing, but the consequences of living in such a world is shocking. I have written a literature response guide complete with open-ended questions and activities which relate to *The Giver*. I plan to use this guide with my fifth-grade students.

4. *Integrated Unit*: I have written an integrated unit which focuses on immigrants. This unit can be used across the curriculum, as there are meaningful language arts lessons as well as social studies connections included in the guide. I have given several book titles: fiction as well as non-fiction; picture books as well as novels. I have successfully used some of the lessons in my web with my fifth graders, and am excited about integrating the entire unit into the curriculum next year.

5. *Mini Research Paper*: One of my teaching goals for the 1994–95 school year was to integrate telecommunications across the curriculum. One aspect of this that particularly interested me was the concept of an on-line literature response group. I found several well-written articles that dealt with

literature response groups and one successful account of a teacher's experience implementing literature discussion groups on-line. I found all of these articles to be helpful. I plan to facilitate more literature response groups in my classroom, both on-line and face-to-face.

6. *Response to Professional Books*: I found both Mem Fox's *Radical Reflections: Passionate Opinions on Teaching, Learning, and Living* and Donald Graves' *Build a Literate Classroom* to be refreshing as well as enlightening. Through these books, I have learned to ache with caring, write with my students, and share my writing with them. I showed these books to my principal when I told her that I would no longer be using the English book with my students. I assured her that my students would be better readers and writers through Writer's Workshop. She has been thrilled with the results.

7. *My Own Writing*: I now know that if I am going to be an effective teacher of writing, I need to write with my students. The only way that I can truly understand the struggles my students face in writing is to write with them. I also have rediscovered my own passion for writing, and I am writing now more than ever. I have included two pieces of my writing in my portfolio: an article that will be published in *Booklinks* in May of 1996 entitled "Jack and Guy Help Teachers Find the Diamond in the Dumps" and a story about my father entitled "The Cigar Box Story." I consider these pieces to be my best writing, as I truly ached with caring over both pieces. I have included final copies as well as the numerous drafts I wrote before I considered each piece 'done'. I use these drafts to show my students how much I rewrite and how my writing gets better with each revision. I have also included my students' response to "The Cigar Box Story." I value my students' opinions and cherish their comments, after all this book was written for children, so they are the perfect reviewers.

8. *Reading Record*: I cannot be an effective teacher of reading unless I am an avid reader myself. My students know how much I love to read; in fact, they often say that my name is misspelled and that I should spell it Mrs. Read instead of Reed. I require my students to keep an ongoing record of the books they've read, and I believe that I should do the same. I have not included all of the book I've read this year, only my favorites. This list helps me set goals for myself. I know that I need to read more adult literature; it is my goal for this summer.

9. *Class Pulse*: I value the input and suggestions I get from my students. I think it is important that they know that their opinion counts and their ideas

are valued. I wrote a reading/writing survey which focused on several of the projects we did this year in Language Arts. My students answered honestly, and for the most part, I feel that I am meeting their reading and writing needs. My students were thrilled when after reading their surveys I have given them more silent reading time. It was a request that I was pleased to honor.

10. *Miscellaneous of Interest*: I have included miscellaneous items which relate to my teaching and literacy in this section. Treasured keepsakes from students will be found in this section as well as published writing that I enjoy and use frequently. I have also included literature from the Society of Children's Book Writers & Illustrators because it is a tool I use in my own writing.

11. *Self-Assessment*: My portfolio clearly conveys an understanding of the teaching of language arts. I have included meaningful and appropriate activities to help children enjoy and grow in their literacy development. I have shown evidence of productive reflection and demonstrated the importance of using reading and writing to satisfy various goals. My reading record and writing samples give evidence that I am a lifelong reader and writer. The items in my portfolio are of professional quality in terms of mechanics and conventions of writing. My portfolio tour explains both what is included in my portfolio and why I have included it. I have enthusiastically attended all classes and contributed to class discussions. For these reasons, I believe that I should earn an A in this class. ▌

▌ This first-year teacher had a sense of humor that could be perceived as cynical, although it wasn't. He often kidded that grading was my job, not his. I constantly offered back the response that evaluation was part of his job as a student, too. Self-assessment and self-reflection are not something we ask students or teachers to do very often. Because of that, many feel uncomfortable with it. This student did think critically about his own learning process, however, despite his jokes to the contrary. I am hopeful that he will give his students a similar voice in their assessment.

Self-Assessment

Well, Dr. Danielson, this is the part of the portfolio that I feel least comfortable doing for several reasons. First, grading is traditionally the job of the teacher. From the teacher's perspective, it is seen as the ultimate time for reflection and self-assessment. From the student's perspective, pawning this chore off on the student seems sneaky and underhanded. It does, however, give the student the opportunity to use phrases like, "pawning this chore off" and "sneaky and underhanded."

The second reason that I feel uncomfortable about self-grading is that I am highly self-critical. It is easier for me, like many students, to see what I have *not* done versus what I have done. I believe it is the hopes of the instructor that each student will "tattle" on themselves and the teacher can comfortably, and without remorse, flunk the student and remove them from the program. Although this is a somewhat highly attractive offer, I have too much invested in this so you'll have to find yourself another snitch.

Finally, I feel uncomfortable about self-assessment, because I have learned in the university system not to condemn myself because there will be plenty of others to do it for me. I *always* give myself an "A" on self-assessment. This means that you and I can verbally duke it out in your office (although I would prefer a more neutral site) if you choose to challenge my stance. I have, although not eloquently, just put the ball in your court and it is you, not I, that must make the final grade judgement. Sorry, but it does come with the territory. To fulfill *my* responsibilities, I will address each item on the grading rubric.

I hope I have clearly conveyed an understanding of the topic. I may not practice all of what I have learned, but I have taken a lot into the classroom. Some ideas have worked, other failed, and some succeeded with adjustments. Language Arts is very complicated and I do not believe anyone could ever master all aspects of it. I do understand it, and I do attempt to implement it.

One of my strengths as a teacher, and as a person, is to relate to children. It's nothing special that I have done, it's just who and what I am. I feel comfortable in saying that the activities in my portfolio are clearly appropriate for children.

Critical thinking and problem solving take time and effort. I will be the first to admit that this semester would have been easier on me if I had operated by just "doing." However, you afforded us time in class and gave me the incentive to strive for something more. Did I strive for productive reflection? I believe that *any* reflection is productive. That I learned in your class. My writing is improving each time I answer your question, "so what?"

I have used reading and writing to satisfy various goals. One of those goals is being a lifelong reader/writer/learner. I love being a role model for students. I like who I am and would not mind if others emulated what I do. I

nt Reading, the time is adjusted in the next session. We want to illustrate that the
ents have a voice in what happens in their classroom.

he following artifacts are taken from an assortment of our courses, over a period of

ral semesters.

~ think class is going
t! You make all of us
valued & unique. You
n to us. I've never had
eacher write down something
student said because they
ght it was worth remembering
tru*ly* *care* about us &
fore, we truly care about
& this class.
I'll be sorry to see
class end, the buzz at
all is ... take Sheri Rogers
                    //
the food idea is
Terrific!

I really like this class,
and the people in it. I
feel like it is the only
class I am learning anything
in this semester, (which is
unfortunate)
   I also think the girls are
cute, and once again I'm
reminded of how good a choice
El. Ed. was, for that reason
alone, (although I cherish kids!)
   That last part was (mostly)
tongue-in-cheek.
   Bye! ☺

3-6
I feel like everything is goodling!
I am learning and have learned
so much already. I feel the
most beneficial thing that I
am getting and have gotten
is your model teaching
style! I feel I have
built my confidence ~~to~~ level
up to a level ~~when~~ where
I understand using Lit., Lang Arts,
Reading in my personal classroom
some day!
                THANKS

Class Pulse

)   What I like about this class is that
its a relaxed and comfortable environment.
I also really like the teacher having to
do everything that we do. (Reading, Journals
portfolio & Alphabet Book) Its to tell that
of all the Education teachers model this
type of behavior.

   I honestly can't think of anything
that I disliked about this class. I love
this class and especially the portfolios
that we have to do. This is something that
Im enjoying very much. The best
thing that I had to do since I came to UNC,
again, its something that I'll have forever.
The only question that I can think of
is the interviews. (What do we need to
know - most important) What are they looking
w. Also, how can I teach a child that
resist want to learn? How can you
tivate them enough that they'll at least
to learn. Also, what is expected of a
ther (discipline etc...) I know it varies
district. I just really got irritated because
m a para in O.P.S. and I hear all the
w how teachers are so frustrated because
apline is such a problem these days or
uld say there's a lack of respect. I would

---

like this addressed because its a
problem in our society that I hope to
see change when I'm teaching. For the
most part, from my observations at the
school where I work, my aunts, mom and
gardma who were all teachers or still
are see that something needs to be done.
This is the only thing that bothers
me about teaching. I love children
but I would like to see more respect
and discipline in the schools. I don't
believe in hitting the child but I think
as a society we have gone to prison
the other side of discipline! I just
wanted to hear what you think about
this or any solution? Hope this makes
some sense. It just bothers me because
I see this a lot of the time in schools.

have recently learned how to read to children and hov

ing during the classroom instruction. Learning about li

interests in reading did not come easy for me. I ha

strides in the last two years and love the direction m

My students always have one to two library books in t

I have provided many comfort level reading books wh

them to read. My personal collection of children's lite

past three years from zero to over 700. Sharing my wri

It's not that I resist writing, but that it is still a little ou

I hope my portfolio reflects professional quality. Al

humorous quality to my work, I find no room for typos,

guilty of this occasionally, especially if I can't figur

checker. (By the way, did you know that the spell

"spellchecker" as a misspelled word?) My dinosaur cc

to my human abilities: four fingers and a backspace ke

I speak. I try to use the English language correctly, ar

"correctly" part.

I have not only tried to tell you what is in my port

what I have learned as a reader and writer. I learned tl

are only small portion of the learning process. By crit

have remained in a constant state of change. My wri

become more clear and more focused. Writing with

process more meaningful. Reflecting upon your own

phase, yet it complicates the process. I don't think I

with my writing because each time I look at it, I see

needs changing.

For these reasons and more hopefully will be evid

remainder of the portfolio, I would assess my grade f(

as an "A." ∎

∎ In all of our courses, Kathy and I take what we call a "class pul:

throughout the course of the semester. These anonymous writing

giving the students a continuous voice in what happens in the cc

undergraduate content reading course, I put the responses to "Hc

you?" in a graphic organizer format. As important as listening to

individual courses are going for them is for something to happen

listening. For example, if many students write that they need mo

10 | I Am a Community Member

Perhaps, more than anything else, whole language is about all learners feeling whole and able and part of a community of learners. It is about belonging and risk taking and feeling successful as teachers and learners. It is about the power of collaboration to break down the isolation of teachers and to establish communities of belonging and learning for all students and teachers.

Regie Routman

We included these artifacts because they illustrate a student's membership in a community of learners. Membership in such a club is necessary for growth as a writer, reader, and learner. The ways in which one feels membership in a community are obviously different for each member. That is as it should be.

The essence of being a member of a learning community is in the belonging. It may be about someone noticing when you are ill. Or perhaps someone asks you about that dentist appointment you had last week. Or you discover that you and a classmate have both experienced a miscarriage. Valuing our unique contributions to a community is part of being a community. The community establishment and existence are by nature bound in context. It's the old "you had to be there" line. And you really must. Because when the inevitable student says, "What did I miss?" in a community of learners they've missed a lot—and they know it.

❙ This first-year teacher was a member of the CADRE program. As mentioned previously, this cohort group is composed of first-year teachers working on a master's degree in one year. This group was very close and learned a lot from one another. This artifact reflects the importance of being a member of a learning community.

So why do I want to see myself as a community member? William Dean Howells once wrote, "I have come to see life, not as a chase of forever impossible personal happiness, but as a field for endeavor toward the happiness of the whole human family. There is no other success. I know indeed of nothing more subtly satisfying and cheering than a knowledge of the real good will and appreciation of others." It is hard to be happy alone. It is relaxing at first, but that wears off quickly. It is necessary to belong in a community. I feel the community of the CADRE is important to me. The community needs to be recognized because it has given me the backbone of support needed to make it through today. I feel that I am a better teacher because of my CADRE community. The support and resources they provide are invaluable to me.

The fun aspect of community is important as well. The summer invited ample opportunity to extend our community relationships beyond the program. The many Friday night "stress management meetings" allowed us to socialize and grow as friends. The pool parties and cookouts are unforgettable. The ever popular, and frequent, study sessions that we labored in to prepare for test and projects. Last, but not least, the friendships made and shared so far are most important to me. I have enjoyed having good friends who really care and look out for me. This is evident in and out of class. Times shared have made the CADRE community the most special and unique thing in my life right now.

C.A.D.R.E. Community

The "C" stands for community. All CADRE associates are dealing with a common experience of first-year teaching and an intensive master's program. Our experiences and concerns in the classroom give us a common bond of understanding and support. I know that I could not handle this program alone. It is a program about community and collaboration. There are bonds that have been made in this program that will last a lifetime. I see myself as a community member in CADRE. I came into this program an outsider. I was not living in Omaha during the summer. I was not a University of Nebraska at Lincoln or a University of Nebraska at Omaha student who was familiar with the program itself, the university aspect, or knowing fellow associates. I now feel comfortable with myself and the program, knowing my way around the university (especially the library), and making friendships that have extended beyond the classrooms in the program. I feel comfortable as an established CADRE community member.

The "A" stands for attitude. I do not see or feel a competitive attitude among the associates. I feel an attitude of cooperation, collaboration, and support. This was clearly evident after a language arts class. There was a class that was very emotional for me. After that breakdown of emotion I displayed in front of the class, I received so much support and understanding from fellow associates. That is something that has meant so much to me, because it showed me how much people really cared. It is really hard sometimes to leave all of my emotional baggage at school. It is something I carry with me everywhere I go. It is comforting to engage in discussions that allow me to release some frustrations and triumphs where people really understand and care. As teachers, our needs for venting and rejoicing are needed just as much as the students. Language arts class has provided that outlet for me within the community. The attitude of support and understanding has really made our CADRE community strong.

The "D" is for the desire to belong in a community. I want to make the most out of this program and my first teaching experience. The desire to teach and touch lives is the one force that has driven me to meet my goals and graduate a certified teacher. It was my desire to teach that let me commit my time, energy, and self to work within the CADRE community. It was my desire to teach and be a part of this community that has brought me this far. This desire has brought about the organizing of our CADRE community. This established community has let me grow as a teacher through the vast amounts of pooled knowledge and resources. I have also grown as an individual. It took a voice in the community to make me realize I am only a first-year teacher, and human all at the same time. That voice helped renew my spirits and my desire to teach. It showed me how to use the community for support.

The "R" is for re-establishment. This, to me, has been a year of re-establishing who I am. I have entered a whole new phase of my life. My childhood days are sadly behind me. My college days of hats in class to hide my bed-hed are now memories of the past. I am an active member of the adult world. I have to take responsibility for my actions, and be accountable for twenty-some growing minds. The CADRE community has helped ease this transition. This summer I felt like I had to start at ground zero, and build up from ther. As I continue to build and establish myself within the community, I have added some extra ingredients along the way. I have added wonderful friendships and memories that have made my foundation strong. I have added a boyfriend who helped me get through rough times. I have gained some invaluable knowledge and support from mentors, professors, and staff.

The "E" is for enrichment. The CADRE community has given me opportunities to enjoy and expand myself. I feel I have grown as a teacher because of the many resources available. I have grown as an individual by the many friendships and collaborations established within the program. The aspect of community is present in many ways. There is a strong support system among the associates for each other and all we do. There is an unstated quest for success and to be the best that drives us. We are all coming from different directions and experiences, but we are all moving forward together with a common goal to teach. We share a common goal to teach, a desire to belong, and a system of enriching support. This is what community is about. ▋

▋ Another first-year teacher, also in the CADRE program, wrote about the other members of this cohort group in another manner, after getting the idea from one of her fifth-grade students. Again, the membership in this community of learners was beneficial for all the teacher/learners.

Erin, one of my students, was absent for a day. When she returned to school, she brought back a book that she had written about everyone in our classroom. As I read through the book, I quickly realized that she had taken the time to say something positive about every single student in our classroom. I know that wasn't an easy thing to do but how wonderful to search for the good in everyone. The concept of looking for the good in people had been lost in my exuberance to correct what I saw as "the wrong in people." May I always remember to seek out the good in my students and my classmates. Thank you, Erin, for a lesson well taught!

The following piece is modeled after Erin's work. I wrote a brief, positive description of everyone in our graduate class. I feel that I know everyone in class because we have built a community of learners together. We have differences in opinions and styles of teaching, but we all share a common goal of helping kids to learn. We have learned from each other because we respect one another and we listen to each other. I can think of no better definition of a community of learners than that.

LYNNE: Lynne is self-assured. She speaks out for those more reluctant to do so. She is also straight to the point. I like this about Lynne.

KIM: Kim is understanding. Kim listens, sympathizes, and laughs with classmates. She is willing to help you in any way she can.

ANGIE B.: Angie is warm. She laughs easily and has a beautiful smile. Angie also has a quiet and calming manner.

CHRIS: Chris is genuine. She is a genuine friend and a genuine teacher. She loves her students unconditionally.

JENNIFER: Jennifer is uninhibited. She pours herself into her students and teaching with unembarrassed exuberance.

SUSAN: Susan is peaceful. She has a quiet, calm manner that makes you feel welcome and accepted.

LAUREL: Laurel is empathetic. She can put herself in anyone's place. She's very aware of and cares about other people's feelings.

JUDY: Judy is trustworthy. I have never heard Judy pass judgment on anyone in the program. She is always interested. Whatever she does, she puts her heart into it.

DEAN: Dean is big-hearted. He loves to laugh and have fun and he wants everyone else to be a part of that too.

ANGIE F.: Angie is sincere. She loves to tease and giggle. She also takes life in stride and sets her priorities with her heart.

SHELLEY: Shelley is a child-advocate. Her main focus is always the best interest of the child. She doesn't know it yet, but she's a blessing to an inner-city school.

BOB: Bob is very caring. He has a gentle teasing manner about him that makes everyone feel comfortable.

DEB: Deb is organized and calm. Her manner has a soothing quality to it that welcomes those around her.

PAT: Pat is thoughtful. He shares his ideas in a quiet but respected manner. He has a warm heart and cares a great deal about the underdog.

HOLLY: Holly is life in its raw form. She doesn't mask her emotions. She speaks her mind. I love this about Holly.

LLOYD: Lloyd is unbiased. He seeks and promotes harmony within the group by reminding us to relax. He is a lover of life.

MOLLY: Molly is reflective. She listens intently and is unafraid to have something clarified. She also likes to do little things for everyone now and then.

MIKE: Mike is quick-witted. Besides being analytically thoughtful, he often offers humor in tense situations.

DEB: Deb is hard-working. She always puts forth a great deal of effort without complaining. She has unending energy.

TOBY: Toby is bubbly. She welcomes everyone with open arms. She is accepting and loves to be accepted.

KELLY: Kelly is always smiling. Only once have I seen her down. Her voice and her manner make me see her as a wonderful primary teacher.

LISA S.: Lisa is full of creativity. She has so many wonderful teaching ideas and she's always willing to share them to help others be better teachers.

LISA W.: Lisa is direct. She says what is on her mind. You know she will stand up for what she believes in.

CAROL: Carol is vibrant. She embraces teaching, life, and friendships with outspoken confidence. She's a loyal friend.

LORI: Lori is friendly. She is a friend to all and an enemy to none. Lori also is quick to laugh and find humor. ❚

❚ This teacher had taught first grade prior to teaching fifth grade. She was not initially looking forward to teaching older students, but found out that she loved kids, no matter what age. This artifact is a poem she wrote about all of her students, showing the community of learners they had become.

This was my first year of teaching fifth grade. At first I wasn't anxious to do it, because I thought I preferred working with younger children. But the fifth graders grew on me and I ended up loving the whole experience.

On the last day of school I shared a poem with them that I had written. I had written a verse about each child and what made them unique. Implicit throughout the poem are inside stories about things my students and I have done this year in school. Anyone who reads this won't really understand it because they weren't part of this community. But that doesn't matter. I wrote it for my students. They are what matters to me.

ODE TO MY FIFTH GRADE CLASS

We call her Stef or Stefanie
her Mickey Mouse bag is the best,
she likes to feast on "Twigs"
and take tape off the teacher's desk.

We all know Tiffany C.
a master of karate she is,
with her ribbons and awards
she can only be called a whiz.

We have another student
who goes by the name of Paul,
he changed his name to Stefanie
but it was only for awhile.

He is best known as the "Sports Nut"
the scores of games are always known
Brian keeps track of all of them
At school, in the car, and at home.

Megan H. can be heard to say
"You know, he's really cute!"
and if there is a boy around
she'll be in hot pursuit.

Then, on to Nick
whose interests include,
"Exorcist", the movie
and drawing cartoons.

During testing one day
she left us for awhile,
and when she returned
Lindsay had a new smile.

David G., the name itself
sings out The Class Clown,
for when you're anywhere near him
you'll never be wearing a frown.

When it comes to Kristen M.
a sketch pad is all she needs,
her artwork is fantastic
on that we are all agreed.

Everyone calls her Sarah
we see her personality shine,
but during 6th grade recess
a new student eyed her "BIG TIME".

Here comes Chris
a violinist he is,
one day he could be famous
and part of all the show biz.

Here comes our pal, Joe
a computer whiz that we all know,
and when it comes to poetry
he'll be rolling in the dough.

ODE TO MY FIFTH GRADE CLASS

When you need a good story
there's only one place to go,
just holler the name William
who's as good as any talk show.

We like to call her Jamie W.
a lover of stickers, that's true,
and speaking of her collection
she really has quite a few.

Those funny noises we hear
throughout our school day,
come from our pal, Adam
whose hands much in strange ways.

And as she tells us all goodbye
and that it's been a great year,
we know her door is always open
as we continue through the years.

* The personalized bits and pieces of
this ode were written by Mrs.
DiGiacomo and then approved by each
individual student.

When we crave popcorn or sundaes
We always call Mrs. B.,
teaching us lessons in reading
she's terrific with a capital T.

Finally, there's Mrs. DiGiacomo
our 5th grade teacher this year,
a lover of Mickey and volleyball
who holds us all very dear.

▌ This artifact was one of the required writings for Sheri's secondary English/Language Arts Methods course for undergraduates. Each week a different student takes notes, and captures the essence of the class session in the form of minutes. Each individual adds his or her own unique style and personality to the writing activity. This particular student was a traditional student in terms of age and experience. She struggled initially with the freedom of the portfolio, but was able to make it her own, as evidenced by this reflection and artifact.

Additionally, this artifact illustrates the importance of context. The writings may mean very little to the outside observer, but to the participants, everything makes perfect sense. The conversation, the compliments, the stories, all worked to cement the community of learners, and the impact such can have on the individual students' confidence.

I included this artifact because it illustrates the bond we have formed in this class. It may take us a long time to get down to our discussions of Atwell and Fox, but when we do, we all know that no matter what we say, it will be OK. No one is afraid to ask a stupid question, no one is afraid to say, "I don't know." As a result, we are all comfortable taking enormous risks.

These people care about me, they value me, they know I have good ideas and they want to hear them. That has made an enormous impact on my learning as well as in my life. I truly believe that I can do anything. Is there a better feeling?

9/22/94

Never a dull moment here, kids. We missed the presence of Jennifer and Kim, but we'll do our best to fill you in. To make an understatement, we had a little trouble getting the show on the road. I think it had to do with the barometric pressure and the reduction in the pollen count.

If you are interested in topics such as perms, hair and marriage will-nots, tonight was your night. Kathy stated that any husband of hers would have to accept her weekly visits to the styling salon. Lisa, on the other hand, does not do garbage duty—no way, no how.

Unfortunately, Patty could not get the gist of last week due to our topic jumps.

Patty: I missed out on everything! I'm still wondering about the bathroom and the boyfriend thing.

Due to her request, we briefed her on the "key-to-pee." Pee anxiety seems to be contagious, as more and more people reached the first step to recovery—they admitted they have a problem.

Lisa: My grandmother called peeing "shedding a tear for Ireland."

No, we're not done yet. Patty amused us with her sister filling a specimen cup story, but not in the doctor's office. We have a new addition to the Guinness Book—her sister switched on the cruise control and filled that puppy right up. To put a finishing touch on the pee thing, Danette ever-so-graphically shared with us the time her son was forced to fill such a cup. The only thing accomplished, however, was a shower, compliments of her son.

I can't quite get into the substance of the meeting just yet, due to the incredible amount of variety surfacing. Kathy returned Lisa's compliment on her dress with one on Lisa's thought-to-be Maurice's sweater. I think the answer was no.

Marty's slovenly roommate with gas surfaced next. Judging by Marty's description of him, he sounds like quite a character.

Sheri kept trying to get us back to the subject. After her third time of saying, "OK!" with greater emphasis, we followed her lead.

The focus of tonight was what mattered to us in the Mem Fox and Nancie Atwell handouts. Terri started us off by saying that kids need big decisions, access to a wide range of resources and flexible use of time.

Sheri added to Terri's statement by saying that a supportive atmosphere is very important. That led to Kathy's rendition of "I Take My Chances," by Mary Chapin Carpenter. Thanks for the musical interlude, Kathy!

Danette was not one of the individuals who confessed her strong pee anxiety, but she is a victim of "lost anxiety." Sheri recommended that all of us get lost just for the heck of it. In case I forget, remind me not to designate Sheri as navigator if we should go on any kind of outing this semester.

What mattered to Donna was that teachers need to genuinely listen to students and read their works in order to notice their capabilities and clever senses of humor.

Danette was in agreement with the fact that unreal writing activities are undesirable and useless.

We all came to the conclusion that "how I spent my summer vacation" papers are hideous things! We felt that choice is important in education at all levels.

Kathy's key to writing is pretending that someone is watching her write and is therefore making judgements. Sheri offered that this vision would keep her from writing.

Bob found meaning in empathizing with the underdog, being able to make others laugh, and writing for response.

Finally, Marty stated that he agreed that only writers can teach writing. He also mentioned that reading and writing teach people how to think.

Closing the night was Lisa's reading of the last paragraph of "To Beth's First Grade Teacher" and Bob's reading of his own piece of work entitled, "Ode to Pollen," which was enjoyed.

Sheri assured us that the Letterman letter complaining about gender bias in his Top 10 lists would be in the mail carrier's bag this very week. ▮

11 | I Am a Member of a Global Learning Community

When people at readings and writers' conferences ask me who my major influences were, they are sometimes a little disappointed when I don't immediately name the usual literary giants. True, I am indebted to those writers, white and black, whom I read during my formative years and still read for instruction and pleasure. But they were preceded in my life by another set of giants whom I always acknowledge before all others: the group of women around the table long ago. They taught me my first lessons in the narrative art. They trained my ear. They set a standard of excellence. This is why the best of my work must be attributed to them; it stands as testimony to the rich legacy of language and culture they so freely passed to me in the wordshop of the kitchen.

Paule Marshall

We included these artifacts to represent the importance of the family connection to who each student is as a learner. The artifacts reflect the relationships that are responsible for the "first" model of literacy these students had. Additionally, this section allows for home literacy to pervade the school environment. Sometimes the most interesting writing/reading/learning goes on in the students' homes, but traditionally school has had no avenue for addressing this issue. The portfolio allows for this exploration by asking for information from this important area of the students' lives. We can't ignore it, and we shouldn't ignore it. Instead, we should give it voice.

In addition to allowing teachers a glimpse of the life outside of school in terms of family literacy, a portfolio also gives voice to who students are and what is important to them outside of school. The relationships they form, the hobbies they have, the people and places that have touched them all contribute to who they are as readers and writers. The more teachers know about their students, the more likely they are to understand their students and to help them tap into their special areas of interest.

▌This nontraditional undergraduate student wrote about who she was based upon her background and what was important to her. She mentions the importance of writing about one's own life, because we have all had unique experiences that make us who we are.

Engaging in reflection about myself results in two important outcomes. First, I look at my priorities and whether or not I'm engaging in the activities that are most important to me. Also, my self-reflection is my insight into how I respond to life in general.

I will be asking my students to reflect upon their reading. How they respond will depend a great deal upon their life experiences to that point. They must come to know that theirs will be different from others' because of their uniqueness.

I will be asking my students to write. Exploring their lives and who they are will give them more to write about than they ever imagined. Their own lives are full of a lifetime of stories, poetry, and other outlets of writing.

If I'm going to be asking my students to respond to reading and to write on a daily basis, I must also be able to direct them in self-exploration.

> I am a middle-aged woman, making a new beginning.
>
> I still feel that my roots are in western Nebraska where I grew up. I'm a daughter of two elderly parents who instilled the values of honesty, perseverance, and hard work in me. My father taught me the value of respecting the land. I have been experiencing the reversal of roles the past few years as my parents age. I have found myself in a care taking role more often, reminding them to get their flu shots and take their vitamins!
>
> I am a sister and an aunt. My role as an adult family member is evolving for me. I'm hoping that I can be as supportive a confidante for my nieces as my aunt was for me.
>
> I am a wife and mother. I am married to a solidly devoted man, without whose sense of humor I might not survive my serious nature. It's a challenge

to sustain our relationship amidst the business of making a living and raising children. I'm looking forward to the day when we'll return to being just the two of us with less distractions. I know that I want him to be my first priority, but often he is not.

My children are my great joy. Having brought them into my life, I feel as if I will be forever vulnerable, such is my depth of feeling for them. Andrew is enormously creative, and intellectually so astute that I look forward to our conversations about his latest philosophies and story ideas. Brian is an artist, a mathematician, and would-be Karate champion. As a parent of two talented beings, I consider it my job to further who they are and try not to get in their way.

I am a lifelong learner. One of my good friends used to tease me about always being in some kind of class. I've always been intensely interested in learning new things and refining what I already know.

I am a creative person, hardly able to keep up with the steady flow of ideas that come forth on a daily basis. This past year I rediscovered my writing abilities and have been directing more of my creative energy in that direction. I am a quilter and love to create the visual and tactile pleasure that quilts bring to life.

I am a community member at school, at work, at my children's school, and at my church. My contributions in some of these areas have been scarce, but I know how important it is to connect with others who are interested in sustaining the important work of these organizations.

I am finally, a member of a larger community, a global one. I don't often carry this vision of my connectedness to the whole of life, but I hope I can bring it to my students when I have my own classroom. ▌

▌ This first-year teacher in the CADRE program (cohort graduate program group) chose to write about herself in the form of a "bio poem." She talks about the importance of accepting our differences and getting to know all our students.

Every person is complex, unique, and multifaceted. It's hard to really know someone just through the interactions you may have with them in one setting. Every person wears many different hats and means different things to all people in their life. I feel it's important for teachers to get to know their students as well as possible through allowing them to share the things and people that are important to them. We learn so much about others when we learn who and what are the most important to them.

In this section I included a bio-poem about myself. I like this format for a poem and I enjoy writing poems so I chose this to include. This would be a great tool to use in the classroom to get to know students because in this poem you write about things that are very personal, like your feelings and fears. Being a mother is the most important part of life so I included that first. Being a teacher is probably the next important part of the CADRE Project, so I also included that. And finally I listed being a girlfriend as being an important role that I have. I wouldn't say that this part of life takes last place behind all the others; it is one of the foundations upon which I build the rest of my life. Without the support of my "significant other" I wouldn't be very effective in any of the other parts of my life.

Bio-Poem

Susan
Sensitive, studious, caring, loving
Mother of Carlie and Danielle
Lover of teaching, learning, life
Who feels happy, stressed-out, excited
Who fears heights, driving on ice, and dark parking lots
Who would like to see every child learn, world peace, and hatred
ended for all time
Resident of Omaha, Nebraska
Collins ▌

▌ This first-year teacher (also in the CADRE program) reflects on who she was and who she is now through photographs. The captions for these photographs have been included as she describes who she is.

I think in order to understand my reflections, reactions, philosophies, and insights one must know me. I feel I have exposed parts of myself throughout this portfolio. Here are the facets needed to understand the person found in this portfolio. The people who are important to me make me who I am today. I am a sum of my experiences in and out of school. They flavor the way I look at the world and the way I teach. These pages show you how I came to be me.

I was: an uncomfortable cactus made from straws, a freshman ready for my first high school dance with my new best friends, a senior ready for my last high school dance with my oldest friends in the world, and a cheerleader who thought my cheers really made my boyfriend play better.

I was: a sorority family, a cheerleader full of spirit, a roommate in my first apartment, a stupid freshman sorority pledge, a college girl ready for my first

Homecoming dance, a weekend road warrior, a girlfriend ready for her first fraternity formal, and a college graduate.

I am: a best friend, a sorority mom, a roommate, a memory of old times, a bridesmaid and never a bride, a co-captain.

I am: a new friend, a hostess, a camera woman, a part of a whole, and crazy!

I am: a very lucky daughter to have the parents I have. I am blessed. My parents have given and sacrificed their whole lives for me. I am a daughter who lives with love, support, and joy. I hope to be there for them the way they have been for me.

I am: a sister who used to think of my brother as a toy doll to dress up, a playmate, a pest, a friend, and a shoulder to lean on. Even though he will always be "my little brother," he is one of my role models. I admire his values and his faith. He is going places in his life, and I am proud Walter is my brother. My life would be boring without him.

I was: a student and a teacher in practice. I was touched by 19 individuals who gave me the motivation to teach. I appreciate and will never forget their acceptance of me as a teacher.

I am: a teacher, a model for my students. I am a CADRE associate who has grown because of the support of my mentor, Mary. I am important to my students, dependable. I am a teacher who wants the best for my students. I am a teacher who laughs during the day and cries at night because I care and love my students. ▌

▌ This special education teacher explains who he is by examining the people and events that made him into the person he is. His honest reflection gives insight into what kind of teacher he is as well.

This piece shows who I am by examining some important events in my life. It shows how I got to be a special education teacher in the first place. I know that I will experience other things in my life that will change my ideas and opinions about myself and teaching. But at this point in my life of thirty years, this is who I am.

This is probably the toughest piece to write. There are so many things that make me up. I believe that at no point in time in your life can you completely know yourself. So here is what I learned about myself in the past thirty years of life.

One of my first memories was throwing a baseball out in my backyard with my father. It was at this time I learned I was left-handed. Little did I know that these two little experiences would influence my life.

Baseball has taught me about discipline and how to be patient. It has taught me about working together with other people to achieve a common goal. Baseball also gave me confidence in myself and did wonders for my self-esteem. I still love the game today.

Being left-handed has taught me how to adapt to this world we live in. I realized that I was a little different than everybody else when I was a child, but that was okay. Being left-handed also forced me to do things with my right hand. This has been a blessing in disguise because I have more coordination than other people that I know.

I learned that we all go through transition stages in our life and it continues till we die. The first transition stage was when I started to walk. I really do not remember this very well, but it was the first form of transportation I used to get around this big world. My legs have a lot of mileage on them and I have not rotated them once.

The next transition stage was going to school for the first time. I had a hard time in school and had to go to speech therapy early in life. I learned that children can be really mean to other children. I always tried to be nice to everybody because a lot of people were not nice to me.

The next turning point in my life was entrance into high school. Of course, I was blessed with having to wear braces on my teeth. I learned that no matter what kind of food you eat, it will have a metal taste to it. I also learned that with braces you get a lot of bloody lips. High school for me was really not fun until my junior year. That is when I found a girl that really liked me. High school taught me some social skills I still use today and it taught me that I actually had talents: baseball and writing for the newspaper. The most important lesson high school taught me was how to get along with other people. At my high school the racial mix was high. I learned that everybody is different and that there is more than one truth in this world. I learned how to disagree with somebody without being disagreeable.

College of course was the next transition part of life. I had now become an adult in society and was ready to find my place in it. College was a big step for me. I learned about disappointment, love, death, and endurance.

Disappointment happened my first year in college. Not only did my girlfriend leave me, but I injured myself so I could never play competitive baseball again. I was thinking about quitting until a girl came into my life and told me I was too smart not to get an education. Jessica kept me in school and made me want to graduate from college. She taught me that I needed to go to school for myself instead of for everybody else. She taught me that sometimes in life you must be selfish.

Love always works in strange ways. I met Karen because I was her waiter at a restaurant. She taught me not to take anything for granted and that people change. The biggest lesson I learned was that the only person you can change is yourself. Karen also taught me about women. I found out that men sometimes do not really communicate with women as well as they think they do. I learned that women want to be heard and they do not like it when you put the toilet paper on the wrong way. I learned to not make fun of somebody because they have other interests than you do. I learned to love and I learned that I must never stop growing and changing as a person. I learned I could cry. Finally, I learned about timing. At that point and time in my life I was not ready to get married and I did not. That is why I still love Karen today and always will be friends with her.

Death comes quickly. I learned about death during my years of college. I finally realized during that time I was going to die. I went through a period of four years that was really hard on me. I lost all of grandparents, three aunts, one cousin, two uncles, a man who was more of a father to me than my own father was, and a close school friend. I was a pallbearer in each of these funerals. I learned that death comes in many different ways: heart attack, cancer, car accident, shooting, and suicide. The things I try to remember about all of these people is the good memories. By remembering good times it helps a person get through that grieving process. A grieving process is necessary for anybody that loses someone close.

Academically, college taught me a few important lessons: how to problem solve, where to find the answer if I didn't know it, how to think logically, and endurance. Endurance is basically college in a nutshell. Do the work and you survive and if you do not you fail. Endurance taught me to break down bigger goals into smaller manageable tasks. Endurance taught me to carry on even when I do not think I am going to make it. Endurance will allow me to graduate from this program

I learned that friends are sometimes more important than family. I have always had trouble with my family and I am tired of hearing that it is dysfunctional. I have many close friends who I trust and love dearly because they have been around me for a long time. My best friend Richard has been around me since the sixth grade. Friends are people that make you a better person and I can say that from personal experience. Friends have kept me out of trouble and have been there when I needed them most.

People with disabilities taught me not to ignore the small things in life. They taught me the importance of life. I learned from them that somebody in this world always has it worse and not to feel sorry for myself. I learned to treat people the way you would want to be treated. I learned to love and not to place my expectations on anybody else's life.

My jobs throughout my life taught me about the importance of work. I found out that if you work hard you usually get rewarded. I found out it is better to pay for something with your own money than to have somebody give it to you. I found if I was nice to people when I first met them, they were nice to me.

Gary, a fellow teacher, taught me how to be a teacher. He taught me to never let the students get to you and no matter how bad it gets, remain positive. He taught me to always try new things and he told me that I was going to make mistakes but that mistakes are good because you learn from them. Finally, he taught me when I am not happy going to my job, to go out and find another one. Why go through life being unhappy?

Finally, I learned that I must always try to improve myself. ❚

❚ This nontraditional undergraduate student's husband is in the military. Thus, she and her family have moved around the country a great deal. In these artifacts she talks about where she has lived and what she has learned from living in different parts of the country.

Where I have lived has influenced who I am. I have included a map of the places I have lived and an explanation of these places. I have also included an acrostic poem of my grandmother's house to explain its significance to me.

Living in different places around the country has taught me that people are similar and yet different. I have learned to be accepting of other people and their ideas and opinions, probably because I have seen so many different things. I know this will make me a teacher who values diversity and who is accepting of all the students in my classroom.

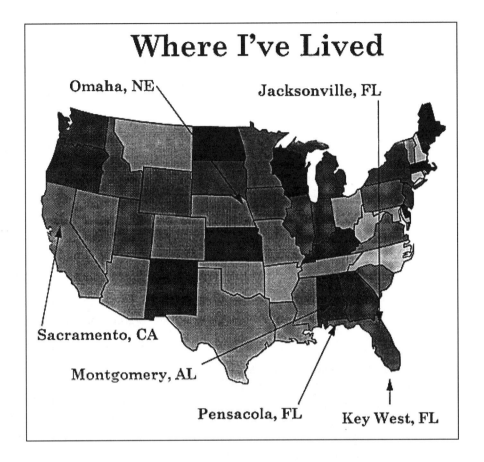

Where I've Lived

Omaha, NE

Jacksonville, FL

Sacramento, CA

Montgomery, AL

Pensacola, FL

Key West, FL

Family Map

1. Pensacola, Florida:

   - I was born here on the Gulf Coast of Florida.

   - 1972 - I attended Pensacola Junior College for a year.

   - 1973 - I began working as a secretary at St. Regis Paper Co.

2. Jacksonville, Florida:

   - 1983 - We were married and moved to Orange Park. I attended Florida Community College and the University of North Florida.

   - 1984 - February 14, Elizabeth Devan Henderson was born. On April 1, Bill left on a cruise for 6 months.

3. Key West, Florida:

- 1985 - We moved here in October and lived on base.

- 1986 - November 21, Holland Michelle Henderson was born.

4. Jacksonville, Florida:

- 1987 - We moved back to our house in Orange Park. After Christmas Bill left for 3 months on a cruise.

- 1989 - Devan attended kindergarten at Grace Episcopal Day School.

- 1990 - Bill left on a cruise and on March 1, Bill ejected from an F-18 airplane.

5. Montgomery, Alabama:

- 1990 - We moved here in August. Bill attended the Air Force War College for a year. Devan went to first grade at Maxwell Elementary School.

6. Sacramento, California:

- 1991 - We drove across the country in July. We went to the Grand Canyon — it was amazing. Girls attended Twin Lakes Elementary School. I attended American River College and California State University at Sacramento.

7. Omaha, Nebraska:

- 1993 - We moved to Bellevue in July. Girls attended Birchrest Elementary. I attended the University of Nebraska at Omaha.

- 1994 - Girls attended Fort Crook Elementary.

Route 3 Box 20

R emember the
O ld white house my grandparents lived in. It was the one my mother grew up in,
U nder
T he giant old oak trees and azalea bushes which grew up to the roof.

E ach of us,

3 girls, my mother and my father remember

B eautiful and unique memories.

O ur own memories, because my sisters and I grew up in it too.

X marks the spot where

2 people raised a family and then another generation did the same.

0 nly a memory now. ❚

Suggested Reading

To read more about portfolios, we recommend the following:

Belanoff, P., and M. Dickson. 1991. *Portfolios: Process and Product*. Portsmouth, NH: Heinemann.

Black, L., et al. 1994. *New Directions in Portfolio Assessment*. Portsmouth, NH: Heinemann.

De Fina, A. 1992. *Portfolio Assessment: Getting Started*. New York: Scholastic.

Gilbert, J. C. 1993. *Portfolio Resource Guide: Creating and Using Portfolios in the Classroom*. Ottawa, KS: The Writing Conference.

Graves, D. 1991. *Build a Literate Classroom*. Portsmouth, NH: Heinemann.

Graves, D., and B. Sunstein. 1992. *Portfolio Portraits*. Portsmouth, NH: Heinemann.

Hewitt, G. 1994. *A Portfolio Primer*. Portsmouth, NH: Heinemann.

Murphy, S., and M. A. Smith. 1992. *Writing Portfolios: A Bridge from Teaching to Assessment*. Portsmouth, NH: Heinemann.

Tierney, R. J., M. A. Carter, and L. E. Desai. 1991. *Portfolio Assessment in the Reading-Writing Classroom*. Norwood, MA: Christopher-Gordon Publishers.

Valencia, S. W., P. D. Pearson, C. W. Peters, and K. K. Wixson. 1989. "Theory and Practice in Statewide Reading Assessment: Closing the Gap." *Educational Leadership* 46: 57–63.

Picture books that model the portfolio process are:

Bjork, C. 1994. *Big Bear's Book by Himself*. New York: R & S Books.

Bjork, C., and L. Anderson. 1989. *Linnea's Almanac*. New York: R & S Books.

Bolotin, N., and A. Herb. 1995. *For Home and Country: A Civil War Scrapbook*. New York: Lodestar.

Bragg, M. 1988. *Betty's Wedding*. New York: Macmillan.

Browne, A. 1989. *Things I Like*. New York: Knopf.

Day, A. 1994. *Carl Makes a Scrapbook*. New York: Farrar, Straus and Giroux.

Gottlieb, D. 1991. *My Stories by Hildy Calpurnia Rose*. New York: Knopf.

Knight, M. B. 1992. *Talking Walls*. Illustrated by Anne Sibley O'Brien. Gardiner, ME: Tilbury House.

Krupp, R. R. 1992. *Let's Go Traveling*. New York: Morrow.

Lillie, P. 1993. *When This Box Is Full*. Illustrated by Donald Crews. New York: Greenwillow.

Moss, M. 1995. *Amelia's Notebook*. Berkeley, CA: Tricycle Press.

Myers, W. D. 1993. *Brown Angels*. New York: HarperCollins.

Spedden, D. C. S. 1994. *Polar: The Titanic Bear*. Illustrated by Laurie McGaw. Boston: Little, Brown.

Wiener, L. S., A. Best, and P. Pizzo. 1994. *Be a Friend*. Morton Grove, IL: Albert Whitman & Company.

Zolotow, C. 1993. *Snippets*. Illustrated by Melissa Sweet. New York: HarperCollins.

Bibliography

Fox, M. 1993. *Radical Reflections: Passionate Opinions on Teaching, Learning, and Living*. San Diego: Harcourt Brace Jovanovich.

Graves, D. H. 1990. *Discover Your Own Literacy*. Portsmouth, NH: Heinemann.

———. 1991. *Build a Literate Classroom*. Portsmouth, NH: Heinemann.

———. 1992. "Portfolios: Keep a Good Idea Growing." In *Portfolio Portraits*, edited by D. Graves and B. S. Sunstein (1–14). Portsmouth, NH: Heinemann.

Hagerty, P. 1992. *Readers' Workshop: Real Reading*. New York: Scholastic.

Marshall, P. 1993. "From the Poets in the Kitchen." In *Multicultural Perspectives*, edited by D. Foote, et al. New York: McDougal, Littel & Company.

Rief, L. 1992. "Eighth Grade: Finding the Value in Evaluation." In *Portfolio Portraits*, edited by D. Graves and B. S. Sunstein (45–60). Portsmouth, NH: Heinemann.

Routman, R. 1991. *Invitations*. Portsmouth, NH: Heinemann.

Smith, F. 1985. *Reading Without Nonsense*. New York: Teachers College Press.

Sunstein, B. S. 1992. "Introduction." In *Portfolio Portraits*, edited by D. Graves and B. S. Sunstein (xi–xvii). Portsmouth, NH: Heinemann.

Tierney, R. J., M. A. Carter, and L. E. Desai. 1991. *Portfolio Assessment in The Reading-Writing Classroom*. Norwood, MA: Christopher-Gordon Publishers.

Welsch, R. 1990. *It's Not the End of the Earth, But You Can See It from Here: Tales of the Great Plains*. New York: Villard Books.